NIETZSCHE

A BEGINNER'S GUIDE

ROY JACKSON

Hodder & Stoughton

A MEI ... E GROUP

ACKNOWLEDGEMENT

I would like to thank Dr Stephen Watson for his advice and expertise.

Orders: please contact Bookpoint Ltd, 130 Milton Park, Abingdon, Oxon OX14 4SB. Telephone: (44) 01235 827720, Fax: (44) 01235 400454. Lines are open from 9.00–6.00, Monday to Saturday, with a 24-hour message answering service. Email address: orders@bookpoint.co.uk

British Library Cataloguing in Publication Data
A catalogue record for this title is available from The British Library

ISBN 0 340 80384 3

First published 2001
Impression number   10 9 8 7 6 5 4 3 2 1
Year   2007 2006 2005 2004 2003 2002 2001

Cover photo by Bettman/Corbis
Typeset by Transet Limited, Coventry, England.
Printed in Great Britain for Hodder & Stoughton Educational, a division of Hodder Headline Plc, 338 Euston Road, London NW1 3BH by Cox & Wyman, Reading, Berks.

CONTENTS

Contents

Who was Nietzsche?

My time has not yet come, some are born posthumously. One day or other institutions will be needed in which people live and teach as I understand living and teaching: perhaps even chairs for the interpretation of Zarathustra will be established.

(Friedrich Nietzsche, *Ecce Homo*, 'Why I Write Such Excellent Books')

WHY IS NIETZSCHE'S WORK SO IMPORTANT?

Friedrich Nietzsche was a German philosopher. He lived from 1844–1900 and is most famous for his declaration that 'God is dead' and his consequent belief that we must therefore create a new man, a 'Superman'. Nietzsche is probably the most widely read philosopher in the modern world, yet he also continues to be the most misunderstood. His writings were almost totally ignored during his lifetime. Until the mid-twentieth century, his philosophy was abused and, especially in English, poorly translated. His influence prior to this had been as diverse as vegetarianism, anarchism, Nazism, religious cultism, and art. It is only more recently that Nietzsche has undergone something of a respectable rehabilitation. A deserved recognition has emerged of a man who ranks amongst the great and original thinkers of the nineteenth century.

Nietzsche was the first philosopher to fully confront the prevailing loss of religious belief in Western Europe with his declaration that 'God is dead'. What Nietzsche meant by this was that society no longer had a need for God for He has outlived His usefulness. Nietzsche was calling for humanity to stand on its own two feet without the support of faith or dogma of any kind. Nietzsche, therefore, was not only attacking religious faith, but also a belief in objective values or truths. We must *choose our own values*. The reason people persisted in a belief in God or truth, Nietzsche argued, was because of their reluctance to face the reality of the situation; it is a form of self-deception. Rather it is better to face and, indeed, to embrace, the temporary nature of existence and the apparent meaningless of life.

His philosophy does not appear particularly systematic, full as it is with metaphors and aphorisms, yet he writes well. Nietzsche was more than a philosopher, for he was also concerned with, amongst other things, politics, history, art and most of all, psychology. It is his style, as much as his content, which has inspired generations of creative thinkers and artists.

NIETZSCHE'S INFANCY

Nietzsche was born on 15 October 1844 in Röcken, near Leipzig in Saxony. He shared a birthday with the reigning King of Prussia and was named Friedrich Wilhelm after him. Nietzsche's ancestry has been traced back to the sixteenth century and some 200 German forbears. None were aristocrats and most were small tradesmen such as butchers and carpenters, as well as 20 clergymen. Nietzsche's grandfather was a superintendent (the equivalent of a bishop) in the Lutheran Church, and the philosopher's father, Karl Ludwig, became pastor for the village. Friedrich's mother, Franziska Oehler, was the daughter of the Lutheran pastor of a neighbouring village.

It is curious to note that the philosopher, who came to symbolize more than any other the rejection of religious dogma, was brought up within such an observant household. His philosophy has, as a result, been seen as a deliberate rebellion against a strict, oppressive and conformist upbringing. Yet the Lutheran Church resembles more the Anglican, rather than some fundamentalist, puritan Church. The Lutheran tradition has contributed greatly to German intellectual and cultural life and has encouraged intellectual and social improvement. There is every indication that the young Friedrich had a happy and fulfilling childhood and he never spoke in his writings of any kind of rebellion against his upbringing. If anything, the young Nietzsche was more strict and conformist than his peers.

Nietzsche's father was 30 years old when, in 1843, he married the 17-year-old Franziska. After Friedrich, they gave birth to a daughter, Elizabeth, in 1846, and a second son, Joseph, in 1848. Röcken was a small village, surrounded by farms. The nearest town, Lützen, was a half-hour walk away and was itself a very small market town. The first years of Nietzsche's life were quiet ones as the family settled down to their existence together. However in 1849 tragedy struck with the death of Nietzsche's father. He was only 36. A year later, Nietzsche's younger brother also died. The traditional family existence was shattered and they were compelled to leave Röcken to the nearby walled town of Naumburg. The young Friedrich now lived with his mother, sister, two maiden aunts and a maternal grandmother. Women, therefore, surrounded Nietzsche, and his younger sister especially doted upon him. Nietzsche's mother was still very young, but she was never to remarry.

Nietzsche was very close to his father and there has been much speculation over the psychological impact of his death upon the philosopher, as well as the causes of his death. Although there is little evidence to show why the pastor died so young, it seems he was the victim of minor epileptic fits and he died from some kind of brain affliction. The speculation that he suffered from insanity is not substantiated, but it was a belief for Nietzsche that diseases are hereditary and that he too was therefore destined for a short life.

THE STUDENT YEARS
When the Nietzsches moved to Naumburg, Friedrich attended the local boys' school. His achievements were recognized there to the extent that he was able to get a boarding place at the exclusive and strict Pforta school in 1858. Nietzsche was studious, certainly, but he enjoyed outdoor activities such as walking, swimming and skating and grew to be physically well-built. However, he suffered from illness through most of his life and it was during these years that the headaches began, possibly linked also to his short-sightedness and the large amount of reading and writing he did as a child.

Pforta School, the equivalent of Rugby school in England of that period, was disciplined and traditional. Pupils were awoken at 4 a.m., classes started at 6 a.m. and continued until 4 p.m. There were further classes in the evening. The school concentrated on classical education – especially Latin and Greek – rather than mathematics and the sciences. Nietzsche developed an enthusiasm for poetry, literature and music, as well as scholarly criticism, which led him to doubt the tenets of the Bible. When he went to the University of Bonn in 1864 to do **philology** and theology, he had already ceased to believe in the existence of God.

> **KEYWORD**
>
> Philology The study of language and literature.
>
> Darwinism A reference to the theories propounded by Charles Darwin (1809–82). Darwin is the founder of modern evolutionary theory.

At the University of Bonn, Nietzsche soon abandoned the study of theology altogether, a subject which he had probably only agreed to do because of his mother's eagerness for him to become a pastor. Nietzsche never really settled down in Bonn and decided to go to Leipzig University in 1865 where he became much more studious.

THE LEIPZIG YEARS
During the Leipzig years (1865–69) there were a series of life-changing encounters for Nietzsche.

* It was during this period that Nietzsche quite likely contracted syphilis by attending brothels, although this cannot be ascertained conclusively. Syphilis was incurable and could result in a life of periodic illness leading to insanity and early death.

* While wandering around a second-hand bookshop, Nietzsche came across *The World as Will and Idea* (1819) by the philosopher Arthur Schopenhauer (1788–1860). Nietzsche became a 'Schopenhaueran'. Schopenhauer's pessimistic view that the world is supported by an all-pervasive will that pays no attention to the concerns of humanity fitted well with Nietzsche's feelings of the time. He also read the *History of Materialism* (1867) by the philosopher and social scientist F. A. Lange (1828–75) which introduced Nietzsche to **Darwinism**.

❋ On 28 October 1868, Nietzsche announced his conversion to the hugely influential composer and musical theorist Richard Wagner (1813–83) after hearing a performance of the *Tristan* and *Meistersinger* preludes. Only 11 days later he met Wagner in person. During that brief meeting, in which Wagner turned on the charm and entertained on the piano, Nietzsche discovered Wagner was also a Schopenhaueran. Wagner was born the same year as Nietzsche's father and bore some resemblance to him and so became a father figure for Nietzsche.

Nietzsche's university professor considered him to be the finest student he had seen in 40 years. Consequently, Nietzsche was awarded his doctorate without examination and was recommended for a chair in classical philology at Basel University in 1869. At the age of 24 Nietzsche was already a university professor.

NIETZSCHE'S CAREER

Between the ages of six and 34 – a total of 28 years – Nietzsche was never to leave the environs of the classroom for more than a few months during the holiday periods. This was, therefore, a period of intense and cloistered learning and it is perhaps no wonder that Nietzsche was to reject a career in academia. For the next ten years at Basel, Nietzsche became less interested in philology and more enthusiastic towards philosophy. For Nietzsche, however, philosophy was not to be found by being immersed in books – which, essentially, was all that philology was concerned with – and he longed to expand his horizons. However, the lure of a salary and being able to support his mother was an important inducement in keeping the philology post.

Basel was essentially a German town, although it rested within Switzerland. In taking the post, the university asked Nietzsche to become a Swiss national in order to avoid the possibility of being called up for Prussian military service. Nietzsche ceased to be a citizen of Prussia, but never succeeded in satisfying the residential requirements for Swiss citizenship. From 1869 onwards, Nietzsche remained stateless. Nonetheless, this did not prevent Nietzsche from applying to be a nursing orderly for the Prussian forces during the Franco-Prussian War. It is quite possible that Nietzsche saw this as his opportunity to escape from the world of books, at least for a while. Also Nietzsche, in his younger years, was something of a patriot. However, he suffered from diphtheria and ended up being nursed rather than becoming the nurse. After which, he returned to his teaching.

Despite his reservations, Nietzsche proved to be an able and popular teacher. Students spoke of his enthusiasm and their sense that this man had literally been transported through time from ancient Greece, such was his knowledge and explication of the subject. A famous incident in class was when he suggested that the students read the account of the shield in Homer's *Iliad* over the summer vacation. At the beginning of the next term, Nietzsche asked a student to describe the shield to him. The embarrassed student had not read it, however, and there followed ten minutes of silence during which Nietzsche paced up and down and appeared to be listening attentively. After the time had elapsed Nietzsche thanked the student for the description and moved on!

By most accounts he was a smart dresser, almost to the extent of being something of a dandy. He began to cultivate his famous moustache that, in a photo of 1882, covers the whole of his mouth. There is another photo of Nietzsche taken with his mother in 1890, which shows the moustache reaching down to his chin!

At Basel University, Nietzsche developed a strong affection towards Jakob Burckhardt (1818–97), professor of the history of art and civilization. Burckhardt's greatest work, *The Civilization of the Renaissance in Italy* (1860), continues to be important to this day. In it, Burckhardt outlined the historical transition from the Middle Ages to the Renaissance as a transformation from people who perceived themselves as belonging to a community, to the idea of self-conscious individualism. When Nietzsche met him, Burckhardt had already been teaching at Basel for 26 years (and was to continue teaching there for another 24) and, although Nietzsche was in awe of this man, Burckhardt preferred to keep a polite distance.

Nietzsche's primary father figure, Wagner, now lived only 40 miles away in his villa called 'Tribschen' on the shores of Lake Lucerne. In no time Nietzsche became a regular weekend visitor there.

From 1871 Nietzsche started to become seriously ill – an illness that was to dog him for the rest of his life. He had suffered from headaches since he was a child, but now it was mostly severe migraines, so relentless he could not eat and he would remain in bed in a darkened room for days at an end. These recurrent illnesses always left him exhausted, and so it is amazing that he was able to work so prolifically. During an absence from university due to illness he worked on his first book, *The Birth of Tragedy* (1871). Although loved by Wagnerians, as it sung the praises of the composer, it was largely ignored by the academic world.

Nietzsche's illnesses became steadily worse, forcing him to spend less time at the university. He was also becoming disillusioned with

Wagner, who he began to see as a sham philosopher. Also, Wagner had moved to Bayreuth, which put an end to the weekend visits. In 1878 Nietzsche wrote *Human, All Too Human*, a quite definitely anti-Wagnerian work which caused Wagner to say that Nietzsche would one day thank him for not reading it. This work, though stylistically a great improvement on the *Birth of Tragedy*, was still viewed as lacking in intellectual rigour or coherency. This, together with increased bouts of severe illness and a loss of students' interest in his teaching, caused him to resign his university post on a small pension in 1879.

NIETZSCHE'S WANDERINGS
Throughout much of his mature life Nietzsche was godless, stateless, homeless and wifeless. For the next ten years, with only the clothes on his back and a trunk full of possessions, he wandered through Italy, southern France and Switzerland. He had been advised by his doctor to seek more clement environments for his health, and this he attempted to do. Despite the illness, Nietzsche now started to produce his greatest and most mature works. This includes *Dawn* (1880), which attacks the idea that morality has any objective basis, *The Gay Science* (1882), which first declares the death of God, and *Thus Spoke Zarathustra* (1885), which talks of the 'superman'. Nietzsche's finest work of all, *Beyond Good and Evil* (1886), brings together all of Nietzsche's philosophy in perhaps the most systematic way Nietzsche ever achieves. Yet he remained largely unknown and unread.

Nietzsche lost many friends during this period, but maintained a friendship with the philosopher Paul Rée whom he had met while at Basel. Rée was also an atheist, but the senselessness of existence led Rée into pessimism, whereas it tended to liberate Nietzsche. Rée would visit Nietzsche regularly and they would work on their books together. In 1882 Rée visited Nietzsche in Rome and brought with him a twenty-one year old Russian woman called Lou Salomé. Rée had previously proposed to Salomé, but she declined, stating they should be like brother and sister with a third man to form a kind of Platonic *ménage-*

à-trois. This third man was to be Nietzsche. Nietzsche appeared happy with this relationship although, like Rée, he had secret hopes that he could win Lou's heart. He proposed to her twice, and was rejected both times. The threesome travelled together for much of the year but Rée, realizing that Nietzsche presented a possible threat to his own romantic intentions towards Lou, arranged for himself and Lou to live far away from Nietzsche. He was never to see either of them again.

Nietzsche became more isolated, spending his summers in the mountains of Sils Maria, a lakeside hamlet in the Swiss Alps. In this secluded, cold region, Nietzsche would go for long private walks while jotting down his thoughts. These walks were punctuated by longer and longer bouts of illness when he would stay in a darkened room. He remained unknown until 1888 when the Danish-Jewish literary critic Georg Brandes (1842–1927) started giving lectures on Nietzsche at the University of Copenhagen.

1888 was the last year of Nietzsche's sane life. It was a productive year in terms of his writing, but the huge amount of work, together with his isolation and increasing illness, resulted in a mental collapse on 3 January 1889. He was never to recover and spent the rest of his life nursed by his mother and his sister Elizabeth. He died on 25 August 1900.

❋ ❋ ❋ SUMMARY ❋ ❋ ❋

● Nietzsche is famous for his philosophy of the 'superman' and his view that 'God is dead'. The consequences of this belief are that traditional values and morals must be questioned and new values established.

● His father died when Nietzsche was only five years old and then Nietzsche lived in a house of female relatives.

● In his early life and during the formation of his own philosophy, Nietzsche was heavily influenced by Wagner and Schopenhauer.

● Due to his illness, Nietzsche was compelled to give up his lecturing post and spent the rest of his life travelling and writing.

● Nietzsche had a mental collapse in 1879 and died in 1900.

The Birth of Tragedy

All in all I could not have endured my youth without Wagnerian music. For I was *condemned* to Germans. If one wants to get free from an unendurable pressure one needs hashish. Very well, I needed Wagner. Wagner is the counter-poison to everything German *par excellence* – still poison, I do not dispute it.

(Friedrich Nietzsche, *Ecce Homo*, 'Why I Am So Clever')

Nietzsche's dissatisfaction with the academic world is reflected in his work. Although he did write some scholarly articles in the 1860s, he was a reluctant adherent to the accepted norms of the academic style. Nietzsche always considered himself as something of a poet and a composer. He liked to improvise on the piano and wrote his own music. As a pupil at Pforta, Nietzsche, together with some friends, formed a literary and musical society called 'Germania'. The society would meet regularly and perform the works they had written or composed. Certainly, he saw his writing as an artistic outlet and indeed much, though not all, of his philosophy is extremely poetic and dramatic. Nonetheless, in his early work especially, this can come across as evidence of an immaturity and a deflection from any kind of rigorous scholarly coherency that would have been expected of a university professor. Coupled with this, his relationship and blind love for Wagner infected his early writing. Nietzsche did not really begin to find his own voice until his split from the composer.

THE INFLUENCE OF WAGNER

Wagner was always a controversial and larger than life figure. Although he had already written four operas, it was *Tannhauser* in 1845 that caused the most controversy. Because of its innovations in structure and technique it both confused and shocked his audience. He was also a political radical, taking an active part in the revolution in Germany in

1848. This required him to live in exile in Zurich where he started composing the famous *Ring* trilogy. The political ban against Wagner was lifted in 1861 and he returned to Prussia. Despite marrying the actress Minna Planer in 1836, Wagner had a number of affairs, most notably with Cosima von Bulow, the daughter of the composer Liszt. After being separated from his first wife for nine years, Wagner and Cosima married in 1870.

Wagner was more than a composer, however. He was also a musical theorist, and his thought on political issues such as nationalism and social idealism greatly influenced the nineteenth century. His music was strongly nationalist and he had also expressed clear anti-Semitism in his writings, making him an attractive composer for the Nazis. Despite this reputation, Wagner did effect a revolution in the theory and practice of operatic composition. It was this factor that would have appealed to Nietzsche and his early belief that music acted as a salvation.

In retrospect it seems surprising that someone as perceptive as Nietzsche seemed to be so taken in by the flamboyant ego of Wagner. It is said that during Nietzsche's weekend visits to Tribschen, Wagner would behave as if he was in one of his own operas. Dressed extravagantly, with only his own music playing, he would waft across the gardens and corridors of his luxurious villa amongst busts of himself, talking mostly about himself! This picture, though most likely an exaggeration, is nonetheless an indication of Wagner's ego and self-confidence.

However, more than this, Nietzsche did learn much from being in the company of Wagner. He recognized the composer's ego as a need to dominate others and to exert his power over them. Undoubtedly, Wagner was a charismatic figure, and it is quite impressive what he could persuade others to do for him. From studying Wagner, Nietzsche developed his own views on psychology, on the desire for man to dominate others. Wagner's eccentricities, therefore, would have been a minor irritation to Nietzsche.

During the early Leipzig years, Nietzsche's infatuation with Wagner and his willingness to sacrifice his own career if need be to serve under the composer, came across only too obviously in his early writings, especially in his first major work, *The Birth of Tragedy*. It was Wagner's writings, especially a series of essays published during 1849–51, that laid the basis for Nietzsche's early philosophy.

WAGNER'S WRITINGS

Wagner wrote a series of works discussing his views on the relationship between art and life. Some of the most significant in terms of influencing Nietzsche were as follows.

* *Art and Revolution* (July 1849). Tracing the history of the arts, Wagner holds that the individual arts (music, drama, theatre etc.) were once a complete and perfect whole. This art form only existed in the tragic drama of ancient Athens and disappeared at around the fifth century BC when they split into their various components. After that time, and up until the present day, people looked to philosophy rather than art for an understanding of their world. Art in its highest and most perfect form is, therefore, pre-Christian.

* *The Artwork of the Future* (September 1849). Here Wagner argues that all the greatest inventions of humankind, from language to society, are a product of the *volk* (folk). The *volk* is more than a collection of individuals; it is the submersion of individual identity and ego and the resulting expression of a mystical group consciousness. The highest expression of this *volk* consciousness is art, and Wagner makes a link between *volk* art and nature. Therefore, the future of artwork is for all artists of all types to put aside their own individuality and egos and the result will be a true expression of nature as art! (This is rather ironic coming from Wagner!)

* *Opera and Drama* (January 1851). This is a full-scale book. The composer sings the praises of his forthcoming opera *Nibelung's Ring* as an example of complete art and criticizes the opera of his contemporaries such as Rossini (1792–1868).

✳ *A Communication to my Friends* (August 1851). Wagner considers the faults and successes of his own previous works and explains why he feels the need for a new kind of musical drama. Wagner presents his own plan to produce a three-part musical drama – the *Ring* trilogy – as a model of perfect art. He advertises his intentions to present this work at a future festival.

This became the Bayreuth Festival of 1876 consisting of the complete first performance of Wagner's *Ring* trilogy. It is a significant event in that it marks Nietzsche's realization that Wagner was not the great saviour he had envisaged. Attending the festival, Nietzsche was later to remark that he found the whole performance indicative of Wagner's German nationalism and anti-Semitism: two things Nietzsche found particularly distasteful. However, in 1871 when *The Birth of Tragedy* was published, Nietzsche was still very firmly in the grip of Wagner's charisma.

APOLLO AND DIONYSUS

Wagner held that there is a dualism between, on the one hand, humanity and nature and, on the other hand, art and nature. In *The Artwork of the Future* he argued that humanity, by exercising his intellect, is actually being drawn away from nature and, therefore, his true art. The fulfilled person is one who is in touch with his true nature and can express this through the medium of the perfect art. Here Wagner is making parallels between the role and function of art with religion. It is perhaps inevitable that when Wagner talks of his own art as being the model for the perfect, he – as the composer for this art – would be a religious 'saviour'.

In *The Birth of Tragedy*, Nietzsche gave a lot of importance to art as a medium through which we comprehend the world. He took on board this dualism of art and nature under the principles of Apollo and Dionysus. These two Greek gods are presented as a metaphor for two fundamental principles.

* **Apollo.** Nietzsche compares the Apollonian with dreams. In a dream you express fantasies but these are a way of forgetting the world rather than confronting the realities of the world. Apollonian art is exemplified by painting and sculpture. In the same way that we conjure up images in dreams, so we do this in painting. But these paintings are only representations of the world; they are fantasies that allow us to turn our backs, at least for a while, from the world we live in.

* **Dionysus.** Nietzsche compares Dionysian art with intoxication. He did not necessarily mean alcoholic intoxication, but rather the kind of ecstasy that can be caused by means other than alcohol, for example through sexual intercourse, dancing or religious activities. Like the Apollonian, the Dionysian is a mechanism for fleeing from reality, but intoxication is not the same as fantasy. Dream fantasies are an individual and private experience where you turn away from the world. Dionysian intoxication, however, is not about forgetting the world, but forgetting your *self* and experiencing a more mystical communal union. Dionysian art is more akin to music and poetry.

Nietzsche accepted that the distinction between painting and music was not always so clear. It is quite possible, for example, to have Dionysian painting and Nietzsche was aware that music had Apollo as its patron god. The more important distinction is how one *responds* to the work of art, rather than the work of art itself.

Nietzsche stresses that Apollo and Dionysus are not opposites, but work side by side. They complement each other, and, therefore, the perfect art (in the Wagnerian sense) is one that embodies both the Apollonian and the Dionysian. Like Wagner, Nietzsche saw this art as existing in Greek tragedy.

Nietzsche's most important contribution in *The Birth of Tragedy* is his attack on the view – prevalent amongst the middle classes of the time – that ancient Greece was so idyllic. Rather, Nietzsche argued, the

Greeks' life was brutal, short and full of suffering. How did the Greeks cope with these facts of life? Greek art, through the fusion of the Apollonian and the Dionysian, was such a mechanism for making life tolerable.

* The Apollonian element was needed to create the illusion, the fantasy, which distracted the Greeks from the horrors of everyday life. If, Nietzsche argued, the Greeks were supposed to be as happy and sunny as they were depicted, then there would be no need for Apollonian art. Yet there is plenty of evidence of Greek tragedy which shows that they suffered immensely. In Greek tragedy we are presented with the images of gods and men, of heroes and monsters, as a way of transforming Greeks' fears of such things, in the same way that dreams are projections of our own fears and doubts.

* The Dionysian element is the tragic chorus present in the tragedy. The chorus would narrate the story through song. It acted as an artistic substitute for the Dionysian rites by allowing the audience to identify with these singing, dancing characters and therefore participate within the tragedy themselves, rather than merely spectate. This was therapeutic, allowing the audience to feel a sense of unity with its fellows, with the chorus, and with the drama of the tragedy, as well as feeling themselves to be god.

THE DEATH OF TRAGEDY

Nietzsche portrayed Greek tragedy as an interactive, mystical and unifying experience that provided a therapeutic outlet for a people who were sensitive to the suffering and uncertainties of everyday life, and in which humanity is in tune with nature. Man is no longer an artist but a work of art. Art possesses form and so by making life a work of art it gives the world a form, a structure. Nietzsche quoted the greatest tragedians as Sophocles and Aeschylus in the fifth century BC. However, Nietzsche saw the other tragedian that is often associated with these two, Euripides, as the enemy of great art.

Nietzsche argued that Euripides rid Greek drama of the role of the chorus, of the Dionysian element. The chorus became less central to the drama, and became a matter of mere convention. Euripides, Nietzsche believed, killed tragedy. Nietzsche characterizes Euripides as a rational man who saw the chorus as performing an irrational and, therefore, unnecessary function. When Wagner wrote of man turning away from art and towards philosophy, Nietzsche saw this as a movement away from the instinctual natural element towards the distant rational capacity. Nietzsche also criticizes the philosopher Socrates (c.470–399 BC), who, like Euripides, emphasizes the importance of reason in the belief that, through the power of reason, we can gain access to truth. Nietzsche always placed a greater emphasis on the irrational and the instinctual and believed that there is no such thing as 'truth'. Great art is no 'truer' than science or religion but Nietzsche believed art could at least help to reunite humanity with nature. It is an acceptance that there is only this life and it is full of suffering, rather than a belief that there is a better, pain-free life.

DIONYSUS VERSUS SOCRATES

In the history of thought, Socrates is considered the first great philosopher. Little is known about his life and, as he did not write anything down, we have to rely on the writings of his disciple Plato who used Socrates as his mouthpiece in his dialogues. Therefore, when Nietzsche talks of the philosophy of Socrates he does not make any distinction with that of the philosophy of Plato. The philosophy of Socrates-Plato can be summed up as follows.

* There is such a thing as objective truth. This was a response to the belief in **relativism**

* The world we live in is essentially an illusion, a poor image of a better, perfect world. The role of the philosopher is to seek out this world rather than be preoccupied with everyday existence.

KEYWORD

Relativism Morals and beliefs are a product of a particular time and place and therefore, there is no such thing as 'right' and 'wrong'.

＊ The true world can be accessed using the power of reason. Humans are both instinctual and rational animals. Humanity can choose to be instinctual and irrational like other animals, but, unlike other creatures, also has the gift of reason. By exercising reason, the intellect, humans can know what truth is.

Nietzsche lays the blame for over two thousand years of this kind of philosophy and the death of tragedy at the foot of Socrates. In particular the whole philosophical concern with **metaphysics**, which Nietzsche considered to be both an error and a distraction from what really mattered.

> **KEYWORD**
>
> **Metaphysics** The speculation on what exists beyond the physical world, such as the existence of god, what is real, and so on.

For Socrates, tragedy was no longer required because reason could remove the fear of death. Although Nietzsche admired the genius of Socrates, as well as his achievements, he saw Socrates as representative of the desire to explain, to engage in argument and counter-argument, rather than accept that ultimately there are no explanations. Nietzsche was not against reason and science – he would be the first to praise its achievements and its role in the enhancement of life. What he condemned was the regard of reason as a provider of *answers*, delivering people from a state of ignorance.

WAGNER AS SAVIOUR

Nietzsche saw *The Birth of Tragedy* as a manifesto for change, a call for a revolution. He believed that humans had lost all sense of purpose and were clinging on to religious and philosophical views that were no longer credible. He called for a return to the principles of Greek tragedy. He devotes the final third of the book to the praise of Wagner as the new tragedian. It was attacked severely by academics although, not surprisingly, praised by Wagnerians. Nietzsche himself, in a preface to the book added in 1886, described it as badly written and confused. However, perhaps he is too severely self-critical. His work has elements of originality and, most importantly, it raises the question of the importance of art in our understanding of the world and our place within it. Art, together with our instinctual side, can also provide us with insights that are not accessible through reason.

✳ ✳ ✳ *SUMMARY* ✳ ✳ ✳

● Nietzsche's first major work was *The Birth of Tragedy*. It was greatly influenced by Wagner's writings on the importance of art.

● *The Birth of Tragedy* argues the following.

  1 The perfect art is a combination of fantasy (Apollo) and intoxication (Dionysus).

2 This perfect art existed in ancient Greek tragedy.

3 Nietzsche blames Euripides and Socrates for the death of the perfect art.

4 A return to the age of perfect art needs to be achieved and Wagner is presented as a producer of this art.

● *The Birth of Tragedy* was, however, largely ignored and can not be considered a particularly scholarly or coherent piece of work.

3 Nietzsche, Wagner and Schopenhauer

> The man of the ages of barbarous primordial culture believed that in the dream he was getting to know a *second real world*: here is the origin of all metaphysics. Without the dream, one would have no occasion to divide the world into two.
>
> (Friedrich Nietzsche, *Human, All Too Human*, 5)

The more cynical critics of Nietzsche saw *The Birth of Tragedy* as little more than a publicity stunt for Wagner. Their criticisms are understandable as there did seem to be some mutual back-patting going on. Wagner, for his part, introduced Nietzsche to his publisher while Nietzsche devoted a good deal of his book towards promoting Wagner as the new revolutionary, and laid the ground for the Bayreuth Festival. When, in 1872, Wagner left Tribschen and moved to the more distant Bayreuth, the relationship between the two men also became less intense. But Nietzsche, despite growing doubts, remained a Wagnerian. In fact, Nietzsche's publicizing for the composer did not stop there, as is evident from the fourth essay of his *Untimely Meditations*.

UNTIMELY MEDITATIONS

The *Untimely Meditations* consists of four long essays written between 1873–6. Originally, Nietzsche had intended to write 13 but – perhaps fortunately, as they are certainly not Nietzsche's best work – this was not to be the case. However, they are important in showing Nietzsche's growing concern with the German culture of his time, and the move away from the belief that the German nation could be the new Greece of antiquity.

* First Meditation *David Strauss, the Confessor and Writer* (1873). This is a polemical attack on the theologian and philosopher David Strauss (1808–74). Strauss' *The Life of Jesus* (1835) was extremely

controversial as it attempts to explain the miracles in the gospels as myth. The book caused Strauss to lose his teaching post.

* Second Meditation *Of the Use and Disadvantage of History for Life* (1874). This is a much better work. Nietzsche, in fact, is not being 'untimely' at all here, for he is meditating upon the contemporary German patriotic concern with its past. Nietzsche recognizes the importance of history in the understanding of our world, but also warns against presenting a *false* history.

* Third Meditation *Schopenhauer as Educator* (1874). As it turns out, this essay is not really so much about Schopenhauer, but rather about Schopenhauer's criticisms of philosophers, which Nietzsche echoes but not as well. It presents a picture of the ideal philosopher as opposed to the academic philosopher.

* Fourth Meditation *Richard Wagner in Bayreuth* (1876). An embarrassing essay in its praise of Wagner which largely echoes the arguments of *The Birth of Tragedy*.

THE BAYREUTH FESTIVAL

After a series of financial difficulties that were only resolved by the offer of a subsidy by King Ludwig, the festival was finally set for August 1876. The small town of Bayreuth was chosen and Wagner engaged in the process of creative and exhausting industry to prepare for what was an incredible musical endeavour. In the summer of 1874, Nietzsche decided to visit Wagner's house. This was the worst time Nietzsche could have chosen, for Wagner was not ready for any interruptions as he had yet to complete his composition for the festival. Nietzsche annoyed Wagner intensely during this period. It may well have been his intention employing such seemingly deliberate tactics as carrying a score of Brahms with him (Wagner hated Brahms), and even playing it on Wagner's piano!

The festival was due to begin on the 13 August and would consist of three complete cycles of the *Ring* trilogy. It consists of a lengthy

Prelude, followed by three complete musical tragedies: a 14-hour saga in total. The inspiration for this new myth derives from a number of old sagas, medieval retellings and contemporary commentaries.

Wagner's stated aim was to present his 'musical drama' (Wagner was clear that this was not an opera, which he considered to be an example of how decadent art had become) to the *volk*, an audience who would participate in the emotional purpose of the drama. He presented a vision of the Greek masses streaming in their thousands into the Athenian amphitheatre, and he imagined the same for Bayreuth. However, as it turned out, the first performance consisted of just the kind of people who would attend an opera: emperors, kings, barons and the upper middle classes. Not surprisingly, this audience hardly let their hair down to engage in ecstatic, mystical union.

Nietzsche, for his part, could have been at the centre of the whole enterprise if he had so wished, but he preferred to remain at the sidelines. He did sit through the first complete cycle, but gave his tickets away for the rest of the festival, the second cycle in late August and the third in early September. Nietzsche was later to write that his morose behaviour during the festival was because of his awareness that Wagner was not to be the saviour after all. However, although disillusionment with Wagner was most likely a factor, Nietzsche's increasing ill health at that time would not have suited the activities of a music festival.

THE WORLD AS WILL AND IDEA

Nietzsche's final meeting with Wagner was in Sorrento, Italy, in 1876. Their meeting was brief and polite but it was obvious to both that the friendship was over. The year 1876 also marked Nietzsche's split from the influence of the German philosopher Arthur Schopenhauer (1788–1860). To understand Schopenhauer's and, indeed, Nietzsche's philosophy it helps to have a brief account of the main philosophical themes that acted as a backdrop to the German philosophy of the time.

The Greeks

Much of ancient Greek philosophy, most notably the works of Plato, speculated on the nature of existence. Is what we sense (smell, sight, touch, taste, hearing) actually what *is*? For example, you see trees and birds outside your window, but can you be sure that they really exist and they are what they seem to be? Plato held that the world that we perceive with our senses is only appearance. Things are not as they always appear to be and we often think we perceive something that turns out to be other than what we originally thought. In other words, our senses are unreliable. However, humans have the gift of reason and it is with our rational capacity, our intellect, that we can determine what really exists.

The view that there are two worlds, the world of appearance and the world of reality, has also existed in many of the great religions. Inevitably, it has led to the quesion of what the 'real' world consists of and how, if at all, it is possible to enter this real world. It is a view that is known in philosophy as **dualism**. For Plato, we gain access to the real world through the exercise of reason, whereas for many religions it is through faith or ritual practice. Plato was, therefore, a supporter of **rationalism**: he believed that the power of reason provides us with important knowledge about the world.

Descartes and Spinoza

The French philosopher René Descartes (1596–1650) expressed this dualism in a simpler manner: there are only two existent things, *thinking substance* (soul); and *extended substance* (matter). Descartes, however, was not overly concerned with which is 'more real' than the other, nor did he address the important issue of how two very different kinds of substance can possibly interact with each other.

KEYWORDS

Dualism The philosophical position that there are two worlds: the physical and the non-physical.

Rationalism The philosophical position that reason, the intellect, forms the basis for much of our knowledge.

Pantheism The belief that the whole of reality is divine.

Empiricism The philosophical position that we can acquire knowledge of the world through direct experience of the senses.

The Dutch philosopher Baruch Spinoza (1632–1677) responded to Descartes' dualism with his **pantheism**. For Spinoza, soul and matter are not 'substances', for there is only one substance in the whole universe, and that is God. Soul and matter, therefore, are merely expressions of God.

Locke and Berkeley

The debate between Descartes and Spinoza took on another form with the British philosophers John Locke (1632–1704) and Bishop George Berkeley (1685–1753). Locke is regarded as the founder of the philosophical school known as **empiricism**. In opposition to rationalism, Locke argued that we are born with our minds a complete blank and so our knowledge of the world comes through direct experience of the material world. There are just two sources of knowledge, *ideas of sensation* and *ideas of reflection*.

✳ *Ideas of sensation* are, at the basic level, when the mind, through the senses, perceives an object or a colour for example.

✳ *Ideas of reflection* are when the mind reflects upon the object that is perceived and exercises the imagination.

The point Locke is making here is that the 'ideas' of mind, whether ideas of sensation or ideas of reflection, have their basis in the material world, they are not innate (i.e. you are not born with these ideas).

Berkeley held that the theories of Locke lead to doubts over the existence of the most basic things that ordinary people believe and this scepticism could lead to doubting religious truths. If Locke is arguing that *some* of our ideas (the ideas of reflection) are a result of the mind's reflection, then why not *all* of our ideas? Locke argues that the 'ideas' in our mind must still have their origins in objects in the material world, whereas Berkeley did not make a distinction between objects and ideas. In fact, there is no reason to believe that there *are* material objects out there, only the mind. This conclusion makes Berkeley the founder of the philosophical school of modern **idealism**. This philosophical position gives a key role to the mind in the constitution of the world as it is experienced.

> **KEYWORD**
>
> Idealism Stresses the importance of the mind in understanding what we can know about the world. At the most extreme, it argues that there is only the mind and no external world.

The question arises, however, as to where the ideas in the mind come from, if not from matter? Berkeley states that the ideas from the mind come directly from God. For Berkeley there are two kinds of ideas.

✳ Those ideas that we have no control over, for example sights and sounds that are forced upon our consciousness. Because these are not a product of our will, they must be a product of some other will, which is God's.

✳ Those ideas that we do have control over, for example reflecting upon our ideas or exercising our imaginations.

Hume and Kant

The Scottish philosopher and empiricist David Hume (1711–76) asserted that our mind consists of *impressions* and *ideas*.

✳ *Impressions* are what Locke called 'ideas of sensation': objects, colours, sounds and so on, of the material world.

✳ *Ideas* are images of impressions that are formed from thinking and reasoning.

We can, therefore, have no ideas of anything unless we first receive an impression. For example, you may have an impression of fire and an impression of heat, you then form the idea in your mind that fire *causes* heat. However, Hume argues, the causation does not exist in reality, but only an impression (ideas) formed in our minds as a result of thinking and reasoning. Causation is based upon past experience, but that does not mean that fire will cause heat in the future. At best, we can only *suppose* that it will.

When the German philosopher Immanuel Kant (1724–1804) read Hume it changed his life. He set about developing the foundation of modern German philosophy that directly influenced Schopenhauer, Nietzsche and all other German philosophers.

Kant agreed with Hume that there are no innate ideas, but he did not accept that all knowledge is derived from experience. Whereas empiricism argues that our knowledge must conform to experience, Kant turned this around and argued that our experience must conform to our knowledge.

For example, an empiricist would argue that if you experience a stone falling to the floor many thousands of times, then you suppose, based upon that experience, that it will fall to the floor the next time. It *may not*, of course, but it is the only knowledge we have to go on: our reasoning creates the 'idea' that the stone will fall. Now, Kant is notoriously difficult and technical at the best of times, but put simply, he asks why do we impose causation upon the stone? That is, why do we suppose that letting go of the stone will cause it to fall to the ground? Causation is not derived from the senses, and here Kant agrees with Hume, but then where does it come from? Kant argues that we humans impose an order upon the world, we impose causation, quantity, quality etc. so that we may understand it. There are therefore two worlds.

* The world of **phenomena** or 'appearance'.

* The world of **noumena** of 'reality'.

It is rather like wearing irremovable spectacles that make you see the world in a certain way. However, this is not how the world really is. The world of the noumenal we cannot see because we are limited in our perceptions. The inevitable conclusion Kant reached is that there are two worlds: the world of appearance that we impose through what may be called our 'irremovable spectacles', and the world as it really is, which we cannot perceive.

> **KEYWORDS**
>
> **Phenomena** In Kantian terms, the world of everyday things that we can detect with our senses.
>
> **Noumena** Metaphysical beliefs about the soul, the cosmos and God which are matters of faith rather than of scientific knowledge.

Schopenhauer

Schopenhauer accepted Kant's view that there is a phenomenal world and a noumenal world. However, he believed that it *is* possible to know the noumenal.

* He equates the world of phenomena with Berkeley's ideas in the mind. Therefore, the world as it is perceived is the creation of the mind that perceives it. In other words, 'the world is my idea'.

* Kant argues that if there is an 'apparent' world there must also be a 'real' world and Schopenhauer equates the real world with the 'I' who has the idea.

Our knowledge of ourselves is obviously different from the knowledge we have of anyone or anything else. We know ourselves objectively in the same way we know other phenomena in the word – that is as a physical object, a body. We also have subjective knowledge, our inner consciousness, our feelings and desires. It is our inner selves that Schopenhauer calls 'will'. Therefore, the body is part of the phenomenal world, the world of appearance, and the will is in the noumenal form, the world of reality.

> **Ideas** = appearance = body and other objects
> **The 'I' that has the idea** = reality = will

The world is a duality. *All* things have both will and idea, even a stone. However, in the case of the stone its will has not attained a state of consciousness.

SCHOPENHAUER'S PESSIMISM

Every person embodies will and the nature of will is to survive. In the Darwinian sense of survival of the species, every individual is striving against the will of others in a self-interested way. This inevitably results in conflict and suffering. Therefore, Schopenhauer sees the will as essentially evil and the only way out of this suffering and evil is the denial of the will, a refusal to take part in the egotistical contest for domination of others. This can be achieved through the power of the conscious intellect, which is able to comprehend the nature of the will and its effects. The result, of denying the will (which is the only reality) and being left with ideas (which are not real) is extinction of the self.

This philosophy now enters the realms of ascetic sainthood and Schopenhauer reveals the influence of Buddhism upon him. Nietzsche, like Wagner, initially accepted the view that we should 'deny the will' although was later to doubt the practicality of such an activity. In fact, Schopenhauer himself was hardly the best model of the ascetic, for he loved the good life.

Ultimately, Schopenhauer's influence on Nietzsche amounts to three things.

* Like Schopenhauer, Nietzsche presented the picture of the philosopher who will stop at nothing in the search for truth, however painful that might be.

* Schopenhauer's style of writing, perhaps more than his content, had an influence on Nietzsche's own style and provided a demonstration that one can write philosophy and also write well.

* Nietzsche adopted the primacy of the will as the motivating force and this became the will to power.

Nietzsche's will to power is in many respects different from Schopenhauer's will. Nietzsche was much more materialistic in his philosophy than Schopenhauer's almost mystical views.

Both Wagner and Schopenhauer, therefore, played an important part in Nietzsche's early works, but this influence dwindled as Nietzsche developed his own voice.

✳ ✳ ✳ *SUMMARY* ✳ ✳ ✳

● Between 1873–6, Nietzsche wrote four 'Meditations'. However, with the exception of his Second Meditation, they are not overly original. He had yet to find his own voice.

● In August 1876 Nietzsche attends the first Bayreuth Festival. However, he leaves after the first performance. The same year, he falls out with Wagner and rejects Schopenhauer's concept of the will.

● Nietzsche's philosophy must be seen in the context of the philosophical tradition he inherited, especially the emphasis on knowledge and the view that there are two worlds, of which one is more 'real' than another. This is a view that Nietzsche was to reject.

● Whereas Schopenhauer's will was pessimistic and life-negating, Nietzsche's will to power is optimistic and life-affirming.

The Will to Power

4

> What is good? – All that heightens the feeling of power, the will to power, power itself in man.
>
> What is bad? – All that proceeds from weakness.
>
> What is happiness? – The feeling that power *increases* – that a resistance is overcome.
>
> (Friedrich Nietzsche, The Anti-Christ, 2)

In early August 1876, soon before the Bayreuth Festival, Nietzsche began work on what was originally intended to be the fifth Untimely Meditation. Initially titled *The Plowshare* this became a book of its own called *Human, All Too Human*. In this work, Nietzsche starts to develop one of the central principles of his philosophy: the 'will to power'.

HUMAN, ALL TOO HUMAN

Not only did this work complete Nietzsche's break with Wagner, it also succeeded in alienating even more philosophy academics. The main reason for this was that Nietzsche was now finally developing a unique writing style. Though hard-punching, poetic and comprehensible, this style was not regarded as the correct form to use for works of good philosophy. Nietzsche started writing in **aphorisms**. Rather than long-winded argument, he wrote catchy passages varying in length from a single sentence to a short essay of several pages which jumped from one topic to another. This style may well be a

KEYWORD

Aphorism Concise, pithy maxims varying in length from a single sentence to a short essay of several pages.

result of Nietzsche's long walks in the mountains when he would stop at various points and jot down some idea or other. Whatever the reason, Nietzsche developed a reputation for writing in a jumbled and ill-considered fashion. In fact, Nietzsche always thought long and hard about the structure of his books. This, more recently, has caused analogies to be made between his writings and the sonata form in music.

Human, All Too Human, subtitled *A book for free spirits,* is in nine books and 638 numbered sections. Although the sections are grouped together according to subject matter, this does not prevent Nietzsche wandering off into seeming irrelevancies from time to time. Nietzsche's punchy aphoristic style meant that he wrote on a page what others would need a book to write.

By considering the 'human, all too human', this work is a work of psychology more than philosophy and it is concerned with the relationship of the group to the individual. For Nietzsche, psychology was not a separate discipline from philosophy, for philosophy was essentially the search for truth. Nietzsche wanted to show that truth lies at the root of our motivations, our language, our history, our culture and not in the quest for some supernatural world in the Platonic sense.

In the *Birth of Tragedy* especially, Nietzsche was more concerned with the problem of group solidarity and felt that through art the individual might meld into some kind of higher community. Now Nietzsche began to feel that there is not enough individuality. In Wagner, Nietzsche found the will to worldly power and the ability to transform this will into artistic creativity. When *Human, All Too Human* appeared in 1878 Nietzsche was convinced that Wagner was no longer the revolutionary because he had been corrupted by success and had bowed to public opinion. Wagner's ambition had resulted in decadence.

In *Human, All Too Human* Nietzsche sees the will to power in a negative way. Apart from seeing it as an expression for the desire for worldly success, resulting in conformity (having Wagner in mind), he also saw it as a psychological drive that explained other kinds of human behaviour such as gratitude, pity and asceticism.

Gratitude

When you seek the help of another you present yourself as powerless towards this other person. However, by expressing gratitude, by thanking him, this is reversed: you are now perceived as the powerful one because he has provided you with a service, rather like thanking the waiter for serving the food. The practice of gratitude, therefore, is a mild form of revenge, of getting your own back and reversing roles – expressing your Will to Power over another.

Pity

Nietzsche criticized the view of pity presented by Schopenhauer and Wagner. They believed that when you feel pity you experience others' suffering as if it is your own, for at the bottom of Schopenhauer's will, we are all identical beings. Nietzsche, however, did not believe it was possible to literally feel someone else's pain and, therefore, experience 'true pity'. To want pity is to want others to suffer with you. Nietzsche observed that the efforts of some neurotics to arouse pity in others is because they wish to hurt others and to demonstrate that they at least have this power.

Asceticism

Here Nietzsche rejects Schopenhauer's call for the negation of the will. Asceticism, negation and renunciation of worldly power are, for Nietzsche, merely expressions *of* the will to power.

It seems, therefore, that the apparent opposites of the 'powerful' and the 'powerless' are merely relative, because they both desire power. They simply use different weapons to achieve this. For example, the powerful give a high regard for gratitude because it prevents the implication that they are the servants of the powerless. Likewise, the powerless esteem pity because, even if they have no other forms of power, they can still make the powerful suffer.

However, in *Human, All Too Human* Nietzsche does perhaps note *one* positive aspect of the will to power; its expression in the desire for freedom and independence. Freedom allows for a fuller exercise of the will to power and is a value Nietzsche supported.

DAWN

Between 1878, when *Human, All Too Human* was published, and 1881, when he wrote *Dawn*, Nietzsche underwent a drastic change in life. In 1879 he resigned his professorship at Basel and spent one third of that year confined to bed with severe migraines. Nietzsche was essentially a solitary person, and he would certainly not wish to be pitied over his solitude (especially after his own philosophical views on pity). He no longer had a permanent address, travelling between Genoa, Nice, Venice, Turin, Switzerland and Germany. He lived in cheap hotel rooms or modest lodgings. Considering his intelligence and connections, he could have achieved world success, but he remained true to his philosophy in this sense. His mission required solitude and a rejection of the distractions that the world had to offer such as a wife, family and home.

In terms of literature, *Dawn* is a fine and clear work and yet it was almost totally ignored. Often translated as *Daybreak*, it is subtitled *Thoughts on the Prejudices of Morality*. Its main concern is the idea that morality had developed out of the desire for power and the fear of disobedience. Here are some of Nietzsche's insights on fear and power:

* Deprivation of power results in both fear and the will to power. Fear is the negative motive that causes us to avoid something, whereas the will to power is the positive motive that causes us to strive for something.

* People are afraid of the consequences of not conforming to the values of society and so they adopt these values as their own. This is especially evident amongst children (and usually remains so throughout adult life) who see the judgement of elders as more rational and powerful.

* Fear can also be a great teacher and provide insight because, unlike love, it is not blind. Through fear we try to understand what we can do to overcome this fear.

* It is humankind's desire to find scapegoats. Those who are weak and powerless look for someone they can look down upon and therefore have power over.

* Self-sacrifice is really an expression for power because you identify yourself with a greater power, for example God. It is not really a sacrifice of the self, but an expression of your will to power.

NIETZSCHE'S MONISM

With *Dawn*, Nietzsche drifted from the dualism of *The Birth of Tragedy*, to a form of **monism**. There is only *one* substance, the will to power. It was now becoming apparent to Nietzsche that the will to power is the basic drive of *all* human efforts. Not only is it a psychological urge that

KEYWORD

Monism The view that reality is ultimately composed of only one substance. It is, therefore, opposed to dualism.

explains forms of human behaviour, it also detracts humankind from achieving greatness by engaging in the lust for money and power politics. More than that, however, the will to power can be seen in a positive light. Nietzsche now saw ancient Greek society – for him the height of humanity – in terms of the will to power. It is the basic drive that resulted in the development of Greek culture, for they preferred power more than anything else. This leads to the following conclusions.

* We are all creatures of instinctual drives, including desire and passion. These are expressed in the form of our will to power.

* The only thing that is 'real' is will to power. Even our conscious processes and our rational capacity are just an expression of this basic force.

* Therefore, all our problems are psychological ones, not metaphysical. In fact, philosophy, morality, politics, religion, science and all of culture and civilization, can be explained in terms of our will to power.

* Not only humans, but also all matter (animals, stones, trees, etc.) can be seen in term of the will to power.

* The will to power, therefore, is a unifying principle. It is realized in nature and history in the rise and fall of great civilizations and religions and in the motive behind cultural and artistic activity. The will to power is behind all of our philosophical views of the world and it is the impulse behind the acquisition of all kinds of knowledge.

PROS AND CONS

If you try to consider human behaviour in terms of the will to power it may provide interesting insights. It is difficult to think of any situation in which the will to power is not present. Even something as seemingly mundane and innocent as a dinner party can possess the underlying principle of the will to power, as the participants engage in debate and conversation, competing for the attention of others, 'scoring points'. Sexual relationships can also be seen in the same light, as can the functions of teachers, lawyers, politicians, or an office boss. Can this be extended to the seemingly 'unselfish' activities? To the person who likes to give money, or the person who likes to surprise others or readily forgives?

In fact, it does seem difficult to ask what is not an expression of the will to power. Rather than to see acts as 'good' or 'bad' we destroy such dualisms and are presented by merely variations of the will to power. But there are difficulties in applying it in the monistic sense to *all* worldly principles:

* Although Nietzsche attempts to avoid the metaphysical, it is difficult to interpret the will to power as *not* metaphysical. The concept goes beyond the psychological because it is everything: the mental and the physical; the animate and the inanimate. In this case, the will to power seems to be the answer to 'what really exists?' as everything is ultimately reducible to it. In this respect, Nietzsche seems to be falling into the metaphysical and mystical trap, which he so much wanted to avoid.

* By declaring that everything is the will to power there is a danger of watering the concept down and it becoming synonymous with 'everything'. In this case, the will to power becomes a meaningless term.

* Reducing everything to the Will to Power does not explain why there is such a diversity of phenomena in the world. For example, is it really adequate to say that someone who cares for another person, or someone who does charitable work, or teaches is merely exercising their will to power and *nothing else*? As with the point above, this reduces the will to power to a bland and meaningless concept.

* Can there be other principles that are not part of the will to power? For example, the will to destructiveness? In history there have been certain figures – Adolph Hitler comes immediately to mind – who, in Nietzschean terms, could be said to be exercising their will to power in a negative manner. Nietzsche believed that a destructive

will, being an element of the will to power, can also be positive. Can a destructive will be purely negative and, therefore, an independent force?

The will to power was developed in later works after *Human, All Too Human* and *Dawn*. It will be encountered later for it links closely with Nietzsche's views on morality and the superman. It should be stressed, however, that Nietzsche saw his views simply as a 'hypothesis', as an 'experiment'. He is not making grandiose claims to be 'right', but rather he wants to break down such distinctions as 'right' and 'wrong'. He is asking the question, *what if* this is the case? Is this useful in an understanding of humanity? Nietzsche was more concerned with being useful than in any claims to be right, for ultimately there is no such thing as right. Nonetheless, this does not prevent a hypothesis from being criticized.

✳ ✳ ✳ SUMMARY ✳ ✳ ✳

● Nietzsche adopted an aphoristic style of writing which managed to alienate even more scholars. However, he was now finding his own individual style and philosophy.

● In his work *Human All Too Human*, Nietzsche discusses the concept of the will to power. He sees it as the underlying force for everything.

● The will to power is not meant to be a mystical, metaphysical concept, although Nietzsche is in danger, at times, of presenting it in that way.

Zarathustra and Eternal Recurrence

My formula for greatness in a human being is *amor fati*: that one wants nothing to be other than it is, not in the future, not in the past, not in all eternity.

(Friedrich Nietzsche, *Ecce Homo*, 'Why I Am So Clever')

Although not his best philosophical work, *Thus Spoke Zarathustra* is Nietzsche's most widely read book. In many respects, the foundations for that book can be found in *Human all too Human* and *Dawn*, especially in the introduction of the will to power. In 1882 *The Gay Science* was published and here we come across the statement 'God is dead', as well as many other passages that are developed in *Thus Spoke Zarathustra*. The importance of *Zarathustra* rests not only in its literary style, but because it contains the fullest exposition so far of his theories on the will to power, the superman and the eternal recurrence.

Zarathustra is a historical character, a prophet who existed around 1500 BC, and he is also known by the name the Greeks gave him, 'Zoroaster'. Zoroastrianism became the official religion of the mighty Persian Empire for around 1,000 years. Small groups still exist in Iran and amongst the Parsis in India. The original Zarathustra conceived of the concept of good and evil as an eternal war of battling opposites. However, Nietzsche's Zarathustra aimed to show that we must go beyond the concepts of good and evil. Historically, Zarathustra represents what can be achieved through the will to power, and his belief that every person is responsible for his or her own destiny would have rung a chord with Nietzsche.

Thus Spoke Zarathustra is in four parts. The first part was penned in 1883 and the fourth part completed in 1885. When Nietzsche started writing this work he had recently lost his 'family' of Lou Salomé and Paul Rée, and he now, more than ever, felt alone in the world. *Zarathustra* is about solitude and the hero of the book is the loneliest of men. Zarathustra the prophet has returned with a new teaching, having realized the 'error' of his old prophecy. The book is written in a biblical style, with the elements of narrative, characters, events, setting and plot. In these respects it is very different from all of Nietzsche's other works and helps to explain its appeal to a more popular audience.

Zarathustra, at first choosing solitude in the mountains, grows weary of his own company and descends to seek companions and to teach his new philosophy. But, even when surrounded by disciples, he retreats once more back into his solitude and praises its virtues. The new teaching that Zarathustra presents is based upon the foundation that 'God is dead' and, subsequent to this, the teachings of the superman, the will to power, and the eternal recurrence.

A BRIEF SUMMARY OF *THUS SPOKE ZARATHUSTRA*
The Zarathustra of the Persians was the first prophet to talk of the day of judgement, of time reaching a final end. However, Nietzsche's Zarathustra gives a very different teaching.

Part 1
Zarathustra descends from ten years of solitude in the mountains and expresses the need for a new teaching to replace the belief in God and morality. The new teaching, 'God is dead', will be brought not by Zarathustra, but by another teacher – a 'superman'. However, the masses laugh at Zarathustra and so he sets out to find followers. By the end of Part I he has a small band of disciples.

Part II
Zarathustra explains in details what is meant by the will to power and states that the highest human beings, those who know how to utilize the will to power in the most positive sense, are philosophers. These philosophers, these 'supermen', will destroy the values that people have

cherished and replace them with new values. They will teach humankind how to love the earth.

Part III

This part acts as the climax for the previous two parts. Nietzsche reported that writing this part was the happiest time of his life. Zarathustra separates from his disciples and takes a long sea voyage, for he no longer needs disciples. In solitude once more, Zarathustra wills for eternal return, for his 'redemption'.

Part IV

Nietzsche had originally intended Part III to be the final part. When he wrote a fourth part he only distributed it to around 20 people. It was added in 1892 when Nietzsche had gone insane and was in no position to object to its inclusion. In this part, Zarathustra's solitude is broken by a series of visitors, including a soothsayer, two kings, a scholar, a sorcerer, the last pope who also believes that God is dead, the 'ugliest man', the beggar, and Zarathustra's own shadow! Zarathustra has a 'last supper' with his visitors proceeded by a speech about the superman. He then engages in a question and answer conversation on such issues as the superman and the death of God.

Many scholars have argued that *Zarathustra* is a better book without the fourth part. However, although the work is certainly more consistent with only the first three parts, the fourth part is very important in an understanding of Nietzsche's development as a philosopher. Part IV deals with a major concern of Nietzsche: redemption. In *The Birth of Tragedy*, Nietzsche argued that humankind could be redeemed through the revival of Greek tragedy and the renewal of German culture. However, as he became disillusioned with the possibilities of art achieving this, Nietzsche still avoided pessimism and he believed that there can still be redemption, that there is still a need to revalue all values and overcome decadence. However, Part IV is less naïve as the ironic realization dawns that affirming life can only be achieved by resenting life as it presently is.

THE ETERNAL RECURRENCE

Nietzsche's teachings on the superman deserve a chapter of their own (see Chapter 6). However, another central theme of *Thus Spoke Zarathustra* is the eternal recurrence. In fact, for Zarathustra embracing this concept was salvation. What did Nietzsche mean by this?

Apart from in *Zarathustra*, the doctrine of the eternal recurrence gets only a few mentions in Nietzsche's later works. However, the doctrine was hinted at in *The Gay Science* where Nietzsche presents a 'what if?' image. He asks what if a demon were to creep up to you one night when you are all alone and feeling lonely and were to say to you that the life you have lived and continue to live will be the same life you will live again and again for infinity. This life will be *exactly* the same; no additions and no omissions, every pain, every joy, every small and great event. If this was the case, would you cry out in despair over such a prospect, or would you think it to be the most wonderful outlook ever?

Though not mentioned specifically, this 'what if?' scenario sums up the eternal recurrence. Whatever in fact happens has happened an infinite number of times in the exact same detail and will continue to do so for eternity. You have lived your life an infinite number of times in the past and will do so an infinite number of times in the future. Like the doctrine of the will to power, Nietzsche presents the eternal recurrence as a thought experiment, not a provable truth.

You do not have to believe the demon is telling the truth, merely to consider the prospect of it being true and the psychological effect this has upon you. Consider the possibility yourself: does it make you happy or fill you with despair? Like the will to power, the aim is to provide an insight into the way we live our lives and, perhaps even to change the way we live our lives. If indeed we experience despair at the prospect of living this life again and again, then it logically follows that we are not happy with the way we live our life.

Nietzsche considered that merely thinking of the possibility is the greatest of thoughts, and this would have an impact on how you perceive yourself, and how you live the rest of your life. This is why he gave it such central importance in *Zarathustra*. Proof is not important here, only the fact that we may consider it as a possibility is sufficient.

Nietzsche's aim in presenting the eternal recurrence was to propose a positive doctrine of an 'afterlife'; one that would not devalue this life. In this way it is much more powerful than the religious view of heaven. Nietzsche thought that the Christian view of the afterlife acts as a consolation and causing people to accept their lot in this life with the prospect of a better world to come when they die.

'PROOF' FOR THE ETERNAL RECURRENCE

Nietzsche was not original in presenting the idea of the eternal recurrence. In Nietzsche's Second Meditation he had criticized the doctrine of eternal recurrence that existed amongst the ancient Greek philosophy of Pythagoras. Nietzsche's criticism of it at that time was because of his belief that events do not and cannot recur within the span of known history.

If Nietzsche did not accept eternal recurrence as understood by Pythagorean philosophy, then can we speculate what Nietzsche himself meant by it? Apart from the ancient Greek philosophers, Nietzsche came across the theory in a more contemporary sense with a writer he much admired, the great German poet Heinrich Heine (1797–1856). In one of his works, Heine refers to time being infinite whereas the things in time, concrete bodies, are finite. He then speculates that if this is the case then, given an infinite amount of time, the atoms that have dispersed will eventually reform exactly as before! Therefore, we will be born again in the same form. However, the main origin for the eternal recurrence was Schopenhauer who considered it to be the most terrible idea possible, an image of endless suffering.

Is this a basis for Nietzsche's belief in the eternal recurrence? The reader must be reminded that, as with the will to power, Nietzsche was not primarily setting out to prove his doctrine. Yet, also like the will to power, it is important to consider the problems with eternal recurrence and what foundational basis, if any, there can be for such a doctrine. Although Nietzsche did not present a proof in his published writings, he wrote a great deal in his notes. However, in making use of Nietzsche's notes, we need to be very careful not to equate the idle and often careless scribbling with what Nietzsche was prepared to present as the final work. It is largely because Nietzsche's sister, Elizabeth, proceeded to publish his notes after he went insane, that people accepted them as his own philosophy and this led to a mis-understanding of the philosopher.

Bearing this cautionary note in mind, Nietzsche's own speculations on the doctrine can be presented as a useful intellectual exercise. Taken from his notes, we can summarize an attempt at a proof as a series of premises with a conclusion.

1 The sum total of energy in the universe is infinite.
2 The number of states of energy is finite.
3 Energy is conserved.
4 Time is infinite.
5 Energy has infinite duration.

This summary bears a strong resemblance to Heine's work. We can see what Nietzsche is getting at here. Rather like the classic example of a monkey in front of a typewriter who, given an infinite amount of time, will eventually write the complete works of Shakespeare. The monkey is typing away in a random manner but, in time, the correct combination of letters will be achieved. Likewise, the states of energy are random but, given an infinite amount of time, will reconstitute themselves.

However, there are a number of problems with this.

✳ Nietzsche relies upon two basic assumptions: that time is infinite (it has no beginning or end); and that the 'states of energy, the matter of the universe, finite. These, of course, are assumptions that may not in fact be the case and are yet to be proven one way or the other. Much of modern cosmology argues that the universe began with a 'big bang' and has a limited time-span. However, it is anybody's guess what existed before the big bang or what will occur once the universe ceases to exist.

✳ It may well be the case that you would live this life again and again for infinity, but this would not motivate you to live this life to the full because, if such a theory was true, it would also mean that every conceivable combination of events would also occur. You can imagine the worst life possible – the most miserable, deprived and painful existence that you could live – and you will live it again and again, *no matter what you do in this life*. Nietzsche can only get around this by accepting a deterministic view that not all possible combinations can occur, only a recurrence of those combinations that have actually occurred in human history. On this issue, Nietzsche does seem to present both possibilities in his notes.

✳ Georg Simmel presented an elegant rejection of the view that states must recombine given an infinite amount of time. Imagine three wheels of the same size rotating on the same axis. On the circumference of each wheel a mark is placed so that all three wheels are aligned. The wheels are then rotated, but at different speeds. If the second wheel is rotated at twice the speed as the first and the third wheel was $1/\pi$ of the speed of the first, the original alignment would never recur no matter how much time elapsed. Nietzsche, however, may retort that his 'states of energy' are random, whereas Simmel's wheels maintain a constant speed. If they ran at random speeds then they would eventually re-align.

It is curious that Nietzsche places greater emphasis on this doctrine in his notes and letters than any other aspect of his philosophy, yet he never elaborated upon it in his published works. When we consider what was important for Nietzsche, what stands out is his belief throughout his life that existence should be justified. That is, the true philosopher does not go through life happily in an unquestioning manner, but seeks to give meaning and value to his existence. In *The Birth of Tragedy*, Nietzsche thought life could be justified and have value through art. The Greeks lived a life of 'Dionysian joy'. However, Nietzsche felt later in life that art was not the salvation he had originally hoped and it was in August 1881, whilst walking amongst the high mountains in Switzerland, that the thought came to him of the eternal recurrence. With this thought came an experience, a psychological impact, that caused him to affirm life and to love it.

This feeling of joy, Nietzsche thought, is the formula for the greatness of the human being, and here he is making an essential connection with the doctrine of the superman. The superman is one who, like Zarathustra, is able to embrace the doctrine of eternal recurrence and find redemption within it. If before and after every action, you were to ask: 'Do you want this action to occur again and again for all eternity?', and you could answer in the joyful affirmative then you are exercising the will to power in a positive manner. The weak look to the next life for hope, whereas the strong look to this life.

* * *SUMMARY* * *

• *Thus Spoke Zarathustra* is Nietzsche's most popular work. It develops the themes of the will to power, the superman and the eternal recurrence.

• The principle idea of the eternal recurrence is that whatever in fact happens has happened an infinite number of times in the exact same detail and will do so for eternity.

• Nietzsche did not set out to prove the doctrine of the eternal recurrence, but rather to present it as a thought experiment and to challenge us to consider what our reaction would be *if* the doctrine were true.

• The superman is someone who is prepared to embrace the doctrine of eternal recurrence and to look forward to the possibility of living their life over and over forever.

6 The Superman

> Active, successful natures act, not according to the dictum 'know thyself', but as if there hovered before them the commandment: *will* a self and thou shalt *become* a self.
>
> (Friedrich Nietzsche, *Assorted Opinions and Maxims*, 366)

In *Thus Spoke Zarathustra*, the prophet descends from his mountain to teach the superman. The German word is for superman *Übermensch*, which literally translates as 'overman'. However, superman – despite the comic book connotations and the possibility of misleading people into believing in some superhuman figure – remains a common translation. Nietzsche did not invent the term. He would have come across it in the work of great German poet Goethe (1749–1832) and, in his study as a classical philologist, in the works of the Greek writer Lucian (*c.* AD 120–180). However, it was Nietzsche who gave the term a new meaning.

If we consider *The Gay Science*, Nietzsche uses the term *Übermensch* to refer to gods and heroes, especially of the ancient Greeks. For him, these were symbols of non-conformity, of those who do not fit within the norm but are prepared to challenge contemporary values and beliefs. This is a theme – the stress on individualism and the realization of one's self – that is evident in Nietzsche's earlier works. A careful reading of these works shows the development of Nietzsche's thought previous to the first appearance of the Nietzschean superman in *Thus Spoke Zarathustra*.

In his Second Meditation, for example, Nietzsche talks about the goal of humanity that must rest with its highest specimens. Nietzsche is aware of what humankind is capable of achieving and raises the question of why we usually fail to live up to our potential. There are examples in history of great people, of philosophers, artists and saints, but even they remain 'human, all too human'.

Nietzsche often sings the praises of Napoleon. Not because of his military prowess but because he represents what Nietzsche calls the 'good European'; the person who is not obsessed with the kind of nationalism that was plaguing Germany in Nietzsche's time. Nietzsche also places figures such as Goethe, Beethoven, Caesar and Michelangelo in this light. However, none of these are supermen, but have certain features that make up the will to power, such as self-mastery, individualism and charisma. Nonetheless, in the end all of these figures still remain 'human, all too human'. Nietzsche is quick to recognize their faults. There has never been a superman, although Nietzsche sees the ideal as a Caesar but with the soul of Christ. Even Zarathustra is only the herald of the superman, not one himself.

Importantly, the link with the eternal recurrence is that the superman is one who will embrace the doctrine: who *can* look to his own life and wish to relive it again and again for infinity. It is an unconditional acceptance of existence, a saying 'Yes' to everything. For Nietzsche the superman is an affirmation of life not, like Schopenhauer, a denial of it and a desire to be extinguished.

It is one thing to talk of a superman, of the highest specimen and of greatness, but what would this 'greatness' really mean in terms of our values? Much of Nietzsche's writings have been taken out of context, and none more so than his references to the superman and a super race. This was not helped by Nietzsche's sister Elisabeth who assured Hitler that it was *he* that her brother had in mind when he talked of the superman. Yet, by the superman, Nietzsche did not mean some blond giant dominating and persecuting lesser mortals. Nietzsche talked of a new direction, but a new direction towards what? What are the political, moral and practical applications?

An understanding of the will to power and eternal recurrence gives us some indication, but to understand what Nietzsche meant by the superman we need to consider his later work.

AFTER *ZARATHUSTRA*

From Nietzsche's notes and letters it is evident that the workings of *Thus Spoke Zarathustra* had been preoccupying him for some time and after the completion of *Zarathustra*, Nietzsche felt exuberant. Although rarely mentioned by name in his early works, the hypothesis of the will to power was always there in the background. This theme was developed in the later works, which proved to be his finest: *Beyond Good and Evil* (1886), *Towards a Genealogy of Morals* (1887) and *Twilight of the Idols* (written 1888, published 1889). It was a prolific and original period in Nietzsche's life as he gradually abandoned the aphoristic style in favour of a more coherent form.

It was also during this period that Nietzsche was as 'settled' as he would ever be. He had established a routine of spending the summer in Sils-Maria and the winter in Nice. He had recovered from the Rée-Salomé affair and he had reduced his contact with the outside world to a bare minimum, concentrating on writing. His health continued to worsen, however, to the extent that he was nearly blind. The fact that he continued to write so prolifically is a credit to his own will to power.

Nietzsche insisted that everything he wrote after *Thus Spoke Zarathustra* was a commentary upon it. However, the superman is not mentioned again, the eternal recurrence only occasionally referred to, and the will to power remains, mostly, below the surface. Perhaps to say that his post-*Zarathustra* works are 'commentaries', therefore, is a little exaggerated. They are works of philosophy in their own right and introduce many new ideas and concepts. At the same time, they do help to explain and elaborate upon the concepts previously introduced, especially in his next book *Beyond Good and Evil*.

NIHILISM

One of the stated aims of *Beyond Good and Evil* was to liberate Nietzsche's Europe from what he considered to be a decline into decadence, nationalism and stupidity. His concerns for the future of Europe turned out to be prophetic and this helps us to understand why

Nietzsche himself was often taken to be something of a prophet after his death, an image his sister Elisabeth was more than happy to promote. The title of *Beyond Good and Evil* can be misleading, as it suggests that we must cast aside all values, that there are no values and, consequently, that the coming of the superman heralds a breed that can do as it pleases, without any regard or concern for others. This, however, is not what Nietzsche meant to express.

Nietzsche's philosophy, in a desire to give it some kind of label, has sometimes been described as **nihilism**. Coming from the Latin *nihil*, meaning 'nothing', the term suggests negativity and emptiness, a rejection of all values and a belief in nothing. Yet Nietzsche could be a very positive, joyful and affirmative philosopher. We can categorize two types of nihilism – neither of which Nietzsche falls into but by which he was nonetheless influenced.

KEYWORD

Nihilism Literally a 'belief in nothing', although there are varying levels of nihilism. At the less extreme it is a rejection of contemporary values and traditions, but does present the possibility of alternatives.

Oriental Nihilism

Schopenhauer was heavily influenced by Buddhist teachings. When he talks of extinguishing the self, and that the world we live in has no ultimate reality, it is this form of nihilism that he is considering. It possesses the following characteristics:

✳ Because the world we live in is not real, our attachment to it is an illusion.

✳ Life is without sense or point, merely an endless cycle of birth and rebirth.

✳ To find salvation we must escape from this world and extinguish the concept of the self.

European nihilism

The Russian author Ivan Turgenev (1818–83) was the first to introduce the nihilist to the novel. In his greatest novel, *Fathers and Sons* (1862), the hero Bazarov is an idealistic young radical dedicated to universal freedom, but destined for tragedy. This novel reflected a nihilism that existed in the latter decades of nineteenth century Europe:

* Nihilists consisted mostly of the younger generation who rejected the beliefs and values of the older generation.

* Rejecting the beliefs of their elders such as religion, tradition and culture, these nihilists claimed to believe in 'nothing'.

* However, the nihilists replaced traditional beliefs with a belief in science. Instead of seeking salvation in the next life, the nihilists looked to a better understanding of this world as the future hope.

The Nihilism of Nietzsche

In both Oriental nihilism and European nihilism, there is still a belief in salvation; a belief that there can be a form of order and values. Nietzsche, however, goes much further than this:

* All beliefs systems, whether in science, religion, art or morality, are fictions. They are merely instances of the will to power.

* This world is the only world, even if it is valueless. There is no 'unity', no 'truth'.

* This fact should not lead to pessimism, to a 'will to nothingness'. Rather, we should adopt a Dionysian 'Yes' to life.

To say the world is valueless is not to say that it has little worth. It does not make sense to say one thing has more value than another, because there is no such thing as a scale of values. Nothing has value; there are no facts, no 'better' or 'worse'. This was a rejection by Nietzsche of the belief of many philosophies and religions that there is an objective world. These religions and other metaphysical propositions often endorse a **correspondence theory of truth**.

KEYWORD

correspondence theory of truth The view that when we talk of things being 'true' then we are referring to things that actually exist in reality. When you point to an object and say 'it is there', then it *really* is there.

This theory holds that when we use terms like God, or 'good' or 'bad' or 'justice', we are making reference to an actual 'God', an actual 'justice' and so on. That is, these terms *correspond* to a reality. For Nietzsche, there is no reality for these terms to correspond to.

AMOR FATI

'**Amor fati**' means to 'love your fate'! For European nihilism, especially of the Russian variety, a rejection of traditional values had political implications with the call for a revolution. For Nietzsche, his main concern was with the psychological impact of the acceptance that there are no truths. It could well lead to

KEYWORD

Amor fati Meaning to 'love your fate'. A term Nietzsche used to express an affirmation of life.

pessimism and despair or the attitude that 'anything goes'. For Nietzsche, he saw nihilism as a positive affirmation of life, to be freed of the burden of hope in an afterlife. You should love your fate without the need of fictions and false securities to comfort you.

Nietzsche's nihilism finds its culmination in the doctrine of the eternal recurrence. People must not only accept their fate and, indeed love their fate, but also embrace this purposeless existence as recurring again and again for infinity. The person who can do this deserves the title 'superman'.

* The superman is a nihilist. He rejects the belief that there are objective values or values of any kind.

* The superman does not, as a result, become a pessimist or suffer from despair. Rather he embraces life and loves his fate (*amor fati*).

* Even when faced with the prospect that he will have to live exactly the same life again, the superman's *amor fati* is not dented. Even existence in its most fearful form is a joyful one.

THE NEED FOR CONSOLATION

Nietzsche has presented us with a picture of humanity and its relation to the world it lives in. This picture is of a people constantly trying to impose an order, structure and meaning upon a universe that has no order, structure or meaning. Rather the universe is in a state of constant change, plurality, chaos and becoming. There is no benign God, no objective moral values, no, in Kantian terms, noumena.

Nietzsche asks why, for perhaps the whole history of humanity, do we cling on to beliefs in God or objective values? There is an obvious need for religious and metaphysical comfort. However, as Nietzsche's world approached the twentieth century, there was a growing feeling that such beliefs no longer had intellectual credibility. A belief in God was filled with too many paradoxes and contradictions – too many claims to truth that conflicted with the evidence.

As more and more people began to question religious claims, they looked for other 'truths' through science, through art, or through Kantian metaphysics. Yet, for Nietzsche, this was just replacing one fiction with another. Having said that, Nietzsche during his earlier writings, notably in *The Birth of Tragedy*, attributed value to art. Nietzsche recognized that art can help to give meaning to life and to gain access to a different way of understanding the world. Although Nietzsche recognized the psychological benefits of art, it was another thing to believe that art is any 'truer' than any other belief. This is not something that Nietzsche would subscribe to.

Nietzsche always took an interest in science as well. He recognized that science provided humanity with many benefits. Whereas religion was concerned with the next life, with salvation and the eternal soul, science at least provided knowledge of the world and might endure the scepticism of generations. Here, however, we can see some contradictions in Nietzsche's own thinking. At times he places a great emphasis upon science which seems to go against his own view that there are no 'facts'. But, although impressed with the methods of scientific investigation, later in life Nietzsche adopted the view that science too rested on errors. Science, like art, is creation and invention rather than discovery, for there is nothing there to 'discover'. Undoubtedly science is useful, but this is different from believing that science is true. This realization, that all beliefs are simply a matter of perspective, is the first step that must be made if humanity is to overcome itself.

* * * SUMMARY * * *

- Although the term 'superman' is the usual translation of the German *Übermensch*, this does not imply a superhuman being. Rather it requires humanity to adopt a certain psychological stance towards the world and to consider the possibility of adopting new values.

- Nietzsche's nihilism is not a belief in 'nothing' and the resulting view that 'anything goes'. Rather, it is a rejection of objective values of any kind.

- Nietzsche adopted the stance of *amor fati*, the belief that you should love your own fate and embrace the doctrine of eternal recurrence.

7 Nietzsche's Perspectivism

What then in the last resort are the truths of mankind? They are the
irrefutable errors of mankind.

(Friedrich Nietzsche, *The Gay Science*, 265)

Imagine you are staring at a painting, and that this painting represents
the sum of all life and experience. The painting, you might think, is
finished. The paint is dry and it hangs upon the wall. For Nietzsche,
however, he is not gazing at a finished painting for it is still evolving
and will continue to do so forever. Most people accept 'common sense':
that there is a world out there, that when you kick a stone there is an
actual stone, that the laws and behaviour embedded within our lives are
so real that they are not questioned. The painting is thick with paint
and it is difficult to wipe aside the colours and shapes of earlier
generations.

Our common sense is merely an interpretation.
This is Nietzsche's **perspectivism**. We see the
world from our own accumulated lives and
experiences, but this does not make it right. The
painting is not an accurate representation of
something 'out there', but the imaginings of the
human mind.

> **KEYWORD**
>
> **Perspectivism** The view
> that we perceive the
> world according to our
> perspective, although
> this may not be how the
> world actually is.

COMMON SENSE

Common sense, the acceptance that things are how we think they are,
is not only seen as necessary for life, but also useful. Nietzsche would
not disagree with this. Our 'painting' of the world is not a random
collection of colours and shapes, but a purposeful process of
understanding the world and adapting to it. Our world-view is
necessary for our very survival. To this extent, common sense is 'true'

in that it allows us to function. This understanding of truth is equated with utility. How *useful* is an interpretation of the world? By declaring that God is dead, Nietzsche is stating that the belief in God no longer serves a useful purpose.

Nietzsche's nihilism, then, is not a rejection of common sense; it is not the discarding of a painting that has taken generations to construct. To do so would not only be foolhardy, but impractical. Rather, Nietzsche's nihilism is a rejection of common sense as really 'true' in any objective sense; that is, perfect, immutable and complete. Truth, therefore, is an evolving process.

If we look for Truth in an objective sense, with a capital 'T', it involves turning our back on this world and looking for something 'out there'; something that, for Nietzsche, does not and can not exist. It is therefore a pointless exercise and also detrimental for humanity because of its deflection from this life. Even though we make this world, and it has no more substance than a supposed 'other world', it is nonetheless the one we are able to live in. In this sense, Nietzsche is adopting a **pragmatic theory of truth**. We should accept knowledge of the world provided it is practical and workable.

KEYWORD

Pragmatic theory of truth The opposite of the correspondence theory of truth. Something is only 'true' to the extent that it is practical to believe in it.

THE MEANING OF TRUTH

In *Human, All Too Human*, Nietzsche speculated that there might indeed be a metaphysical world, but at the very best this is just a bare possibility and much too inadequate to look to it for salvation. Here, however, there seems to be an inconsistency in Nietzsche's thought: is there a 'real' world or isn't there? Truth, for Nietzsche, seems to be equated with 'workable fictions'; yet he also seems to want to say what the world is actually *like*. Here he becomes muddled, on the one hand declaring that the world is a matter of perspective, whilst on the other hand not entirely denying the possibility that we can have endurable facts. As an example, it is a 'fact' that humans need oxygen to breathe. Are we to say that this is a matter merely of perspective? A 'truth' that we need to survive, but that we cannot say that '*there really is oxygen, and we really need it*'? Are we then presented with a hierarchy of knowledge, some 'truer' than others?

Even if Nietzsche were to say, as he certainly seems to, that our understanding of the world all boils down to aspects of the will to power, there is a danger here of introducing his own metaphysics: a 'force' that prevails across the universe.

REASON AND THE SENSES

Nietzsche was frequently given the title not only of a nihilist, but also an irrationalist. However, he was not against reason. What Nietzsche was against was anything that is not useful, anything that makes life impossible. His criticism was not against reason, but against rationalist philosophers such as Plato. Plato emphasized reason at the expense of the senses and this world. His rationalism took him into another realm, a belief in rational truth. As a result, Plato considered this world an illusion and a distraction from rational meditation. The senses can give us grounds for belief, but never true knowledge.

Nietzsche held that reason couldn't be accepted at the expense or neglect of the senses. Even in his later work, *The Twilight of the Idols* (1889), Nietzsche continued to hold that the senses allow us to sharpen our beliefs and teaches us to think. Nietzsche here is not being irrational in an emotive, animal sense. Although he believed that the passions are important and that they can teach us, he saw the role of the senses as an educational tool that enables us to observe the world and fine-tune our perspective of it.

THE IMPORTANCE OF LANGUAGE

If we consider the history of thought we become aware that this history is almost entirely a belief in gods or a God, an afterlife, and the eternal soul. It is only very recently, a small fraction of this timeline, that people have begun to question these concepts. Now, returning to our painting once more: if every brush stroke represents a hundred years of the history of mankind, then the questioning of metaphysical concepts amounts to only one such brushstroke, hidden amongst thousands of others. If our world-view is painted in such a way, Nietzsche also asserted that so is our language. In *Twilight of the Idols*, Nietzsche famously declared that we would not get rid of God until we get rid of grammar. This view was echoed later by the British philosopher Bertrand Russell (1872–1970) who believed that everyday language embodies the metaphysics of the Stone Age. If we are to establish a better philosophy then we must work out a new language.

Nietzsche argues that the language we speak seduces people. When people use terms such as 'mind' or 'soul' it is so embedded within our language that, as Nietzsche says, we would rather break a bone in our body than break a word. Most of our language is based upon early humankind, upon a more primitive psychology that we cannot escape from because of our use of everyday language. When we use a word we still remain attached to the common sense view that the word actually refers to something, rather than it being the product of humankind many generations ago.

Our attachment to our language is so strong that we could not readily do without the fictions it describes. Nietzsche also believed that even the language of physics is a fiction, an interpretation to suit us. He talks of the concept of atoms as a useful tool to explain the nature of the universe, but that is all that they are. However, Nietzsche's perspectivism goes much further than this for it is not just theoretical entities such as atoms, but all entities that are fictions. All bodies, lines, surfaces, concepts of cause and effect and of motion; these are all just articles of faith but do not in themselves constitute a proof.

Nietzsche asks why it is necessary to believe in such concepts as cause and effect. He does not entirely accept the Kantian view that we have 'human spectacles' and that we therefore have no choice but to perceive the world in a certain way. Rather we have learnt through harsh experience that the way we perceive the world is the most suitable for survival. There may well have been many people who have seen the world in a different way but, as a consequence, have perished.

The view of causality that Nietzsche presents is not very different from Hume's. Hume argued that we arrive at the concept of cause and effect not because causality actually exists in nature, but because, through habit, we conjoin one event with another. Therefore, causality is a product of the mind, but a necessary product nonetheless. For Nietzsche they are conventional fictions that are useful for communication.

There have been philosophers and scientists who have also rejected the world of 'common sense', but Nietzsche asserts that they then make the mistake of creating another world that they consider to be real. Despite Nietzsche's charity towards science, he does not accept that it has brought us any closer to reality because, for Nietzsche, there is no reality. Since the time of Galileo in the seventeenth century, it has been the practice of scientists to present theories that conflict with the contemporary common sense view of the world. For example the view that the earth revolves around the sun, or that humanity evolved from other species. This has resulted in often radical transformations in our understanding of the world and led to a new common sense view. For the scientist, these theories are usually regarded as allowing us to get closer to how the universe really is. For Nietzsche, despite their pragmatic application, they are still nonetheless a fiction. They are no more 'real' than other world-views.

THOUGHTS ABOUT THE 'REAL' WORLD

Nietzsche could never persuade himself to adopt the stance of philosophical idealism: the view that there is no world outside the mind at all. This is because Nietzsche did believe that there is a world out there, but a world so different, so unwilling to conform to our desire for an ordered and structured universe, that it is impossible to even conceive of this world, let alone talk about it. Nietzsche, therefore, does not entirely escape from Kant's clutches and, as he grew older, he speculated more about this 'real' world.

Inevitably, as soon as one attempts to talk about the 'real' world we are immediately tongue-tied by the limitations of our language. Because we have no other language we are sucked into using metaphysical terms that tie us to our world-view. Although we may not have any other language, we can perhaps play with language. Certainly, Nietzsche's aphoristic style, his clever play on words, his confrontational and controversial idiom, forces us to question and think. Not unlike mystical traditions that employ poetry, riddles, *koans* and so on in an attempt to describe the indescribable, Nietzsche is also compelled to use similar methods. This may well give his philosophy a 'mystical' quality, but this perhaps is unavoidable.

Does Nietzsche's perspectivism help to provide us with a clearer understanding of the Superman? Nietzsche's *Übermensch* would not be deluded into believing in a reality that can be attained or comprehended, nor would he look to religion or traditional philosophy for salvation. He would be less concerned with stating what is true than in telling what is false. Yet he would also need to have a common sense perspective if he is to survive; the extreme sceptic would not be able to get out of bed in the mornings. However, this should not prevent daring experimentation in seeking a new language and philosophy. Would Nietzsche go so far as to suggest a *physical* change also? Is he pre-empting the advances in genetic engineering? This, one suspects, would be giving the German philosopher too much credit.

❋ ❋ ❋ SUMMARY ❋ ❋ ❋

● Nietzsche believed that there is no 'true' way of seeing the world. It is all a matter of perspective. What matters is whether our view of the world is useful or not.

● Nietzsche did not reject reason, but could not accept it at the expense of the senses or the passions.

● He recognized the importance of language in structuring the way we perceive the world.

● He was not an idealist for he believed that there is a real world out there, but that we are unable to say anything about it and it is a waste of time to even speculate upon it.

The Master-Slave Morality and the Death of God

God is dead. God remains dead. And we have killed him.

(Friedrich Nietzsche, *The Gay Science*, 125)

Nietzsche is not so much concerned with the fact that our beliefs are false, but rather the belief *about* these beliefs. That is, why should we hold the beliefs that we do? At the beginning of Nietzsche's epitome *Beyond Good and Evil*, he raises the question of why we want truth, why not *untruth*? It is frequently the career of philosophers to seek for truth, and Nietzsche targets them for his main criticism. The most important question should not be what is true or not, but the extent to which a belief supports life and maintains a species. When philosophers make claims to truth they are merely presenting a preconceived dogma that tells you more about the philosopher's beliefs than anything to do with truths. For Nietzsche, this is especially true of moral philosophy – the attempt to make a science of morals, to establish an objective morality.

Nietzsche first declares that God is dead in *The Gay Science*. By this, Nietzsche means that society no longer has a use for God. The belief does not in any way help the survival of the species, rather it hinders. The implications of this are important for ethics. With the death of God comes the death of religious, especially Christian, morality – a morality that has underpinned Western culture since the fourth century.

THE GENEALOGY OF MORALS

The title of Nietzsche's fine work *The Genealogy of Morals* (1887) conveys exactly the intentions of the book – to consider the ancestry of our morality. The fact that Nietzsche claims our morality has a traceable evolved ancestry at all would have shocked many a reader in his time. Morals were seen as given by the divine lawgiver God and so there is no genealogy to trace. If the lawgiver disappears, then so does the law and the fear of moral anarchy will result. Yet Nietzsche argues that morality can be explained in naturalistic terms, without the need for a God or gods. Morals are natural phenomena that have evolved as a result of the need to keep societies together and to check instinctual drives that would destroy the unity of the group if they were allowed free reign. Therefore, morality is a result of circumstance, but it is the circumstance that comes first followed by morality, not the other way around.

For Nietzsche, morality:

* is a result of circumstance, not the other way around;
* serves a useful function of binding the fabric of the group;
* can, however, outlive its use and become a hindering custom.

If morality ceases to serve a useful function and yet continues to be maintained by society, this might stunt the growth of that society because it continues to live by rules that are no longer applicable to it. Nietzsche looked to his own society and saw it to be in a state of decay for the very reason that it looks to the old values; the old *Christian* values. What was needed is a *new morality*. By considering the genealogy of morals Nietzsche hoped to demonstrate why we have the values that we do. This way, if we still continue to hold such values we are at least aware that they are effectively redundant. Nietzsche's ultimate hope is that we, or perhaps the Superman, will create new values.

THE ROLE OF RELIGION

Why, Nietzsche wonders, haven't people woken up to the fact that God is dead? He puts this down to the instrumental role of religion. It is the *function* of religion that Nietzsche is concerned with, not its truth or falsity. Nietzsche, like the German sociologist and philosopher Karl Marx (1818–83), considered religion to have a sociological foundation.

* Religion originates in primitive societies.

* These societies, frightened by the forces of nature, personalized them by creating gods.

* As a way of placating or controlling nature, people would worship and give sacrifices to the gods.

* In this way, religious ritual became established, although they were really no more than human constructs.

Christianity too was the result of a human need. In considering why Christianity originates with the slaves of the Roman Empire, Nietzsche argued that they saw this as a way of release from bondage. As the slaves were not powerful enough to literally free themselves from their masters, they were consoled by religious belief that provided them with spiritual liberation.

'RESSENTIMENT'

Christianity, like everything else, is an expression of the will to power. The first Christians were slaves under the Roman Empire and so the only way they could assert any kind of superiority over the Romans was to assume a higher spiritual status. This was achieved, according to Nietzsche, by inverting the values of society. For example, values such as compassion or pity were regarded by Christians as righteous values that would lead to reward from God, whereas other values such as self-interest were seen as sinful. Remember Nietzsche argued that the expression of pity is a weapon the weak use against the strong.

The real motive for promoting such values was not that there is a God to enforce such values, but because the slaves resented the status of the Romans and wanted to possess their power. This is what Nietzsche means by the French term **ressentiment**. The slave feels relatively impotent compared with the master and he is not able to accept the idea that he is treated

KEYWORD

Ressentiment The French word for 'resentment'. Nietzsche uses it to explain his genealogy of morals. *Ressentiment* is the hostility that the slave feels towards the master.

worse than others. This leads to hostility, to resentment, yet he is unable to release this hostility because of his enslavement. What is the slave to do? He cannot simply use brute force, as this will result in him being in a worse state than before, and so he must use guile.

In order to enact revenge upon his master, the slave uses the weapon of moral conduct. It consists of getting the master to acquiesce to the moral code of the slave and, as a result, appraise himself according to the slave's perspective. As Christians, of course, the slaves should not have the option of revenge, for they should 'turn the other cheek'. However, so successful were the slaves in their guile and secrecy they managed to disguise their revenge under the cloak of pure intentions.

As the master estimates his own worth according to the values of the slave he will perceive himself and his actions as evil and reprehensible. His old aristocratic values are discarded, as he feels morally obliged to do 'good' in the Christian sense. Nietzsche portrays the Roman aristocrat as physically powerful, healthy and aggressive. These qualities remain but, unable to express them internally, they are directed inwards. The aristocrat ends up punishing himself rather than others.

THE MASTER-SLAVE MORALITY

For Nietzsche, slave morality could only arise out of hatred and fear. The slave's morality is a reaction to the actions of others. That is, when someone does something to you that you resent, then you class it as 'bad' and, consequently, you create a morality in opposition to this that is 'good'. If you are frightened of your neighbour you react by wanting your neighbour to love you and this is why love is a Christian virtue.

The master morality, however, is not a reaction to others at all. The masters have no need to view themselves according to the actions of others, but rather affirm themselves. They do not need to be loved or for everyone to conform. The masters can also hate, but this hatred is discharged in a 'healthy' manner through direct action, rather than, in the case of the weak, through resentment.

Nietzsche is presenting both an historical and psychological portrayal, and it is dubious on both counts. From the psychological point of view, Nietzsche portrays the slave as someone with so much pent-up aggression that it becomes poisonous unless it is expressed in some 'natural' way. This resembles the equally questionable psychological theory that children should be allowed to let out their aggression otherwise it will remain bottled up inside and express itself in later life in some other form.

From the historical perspective we must allow Nietzsche a certain degree of artistic licence so long as the point is made. Nietzsche is specifically thinking of Christianity when he talks of religion. Nietzsche was not talking about all religions, for he admired the Greek religion. His main concern with Christianity was its dehumanization. Because God is regarded so highly, as perfect and all-good in fact, then it logically follows that the human regards himself as lowly, as necessarily imperfect and sinful. Nietzsche did also criticize Jewish slave-morality for being the originator of Christian morality.

One of the misunderstandings of Nietzsche's philosophy needs to be made clear at this point. Nietzsche was not an anti-Semite. It is clear from his correspondence that he hated anti-Semites and, in fact, all racist theories. This misunderstanding derives from reading Nietzsche out of context, always a dangerous thing to do, as well as Nietzsche's youthful enthusiasm for Wagner's ideas. Wagner was most definitely an anti-Semite. Nietzsche's sister Elizabeth, who married an anti-Semite, interpreted her brother's works as anti-Jewish. Nietzsche's language can be easily misinterpreted, especially when he uses such phrases as 'blond beast' when referring to the masters. This has been used as an indication that Nietzsche supported German nationalism and Hitler's views on Aryanism. However, what Nietzsche actually meant by 'blond beast' was a reference to the lion as king of beasts.

Nonetheless, Nietzsche's views on the master-slave morality are perhaps his most controversial and it is easy to understand why this is the case when a few of the main points are considered.

* The master morality made a distinction between 'good' and 'bad'. 'Good' applies to the masters who are united, noble and strong. 'Bad' refers to the slaves who are weak and base.

* This notion of 'good' and 'bad' therefore is *not* moral. 'Bad' merely meant to be one of the herd, the 'low-minded'. 'Good' meant the noble and intellectual.

* Christianity re-interpreted 'good' and 'bad' as 'good' and 'evil'. 'Good' was now represented by the life and teaching of Jesus Christ, by values such as altruism. 'Evil' became what was previously 'bad' for the masters.

Nietzsche obviously admires the 'masters' and there is a certain pro-aristocracy element to him here. Nietzsche evidently approves of a clearly defined class structure and had a disdain for the moral and social mores of the masses. He was certainly very conservative in this respect and was no liberal democrat!

THE PRIESTS

Nietzsche specifically attacks the Christian priests in their role of promoting the slave morality. The priests were in a unique position in society. They were both strong and weak at the same time. They were weak in relation to the aristocratic masters, but they were strong spiritually because they were God's agents on earth. The pastoral, as opposed to the royal, power that the priests possessed was used as a tool for social control and promoting the moral ideal of the herd.

Although he refers to the herd, or slave, morality as promoting the teachings of Christ, Nietzsche places the blame firmly on St Paul as the one who misinterpreted Jesus' teachings. In fact, Nietzsche regards Jesus as a member of the master morality because Jesus was a life affirmer who criticized the Jewish priests for using religion as a means of social control. St Paul, who travelled across the Roman Empire establishing churches in the first century, set the stage for the development of the slave morality and corrupted Jesus' teachings to suit his own ends. The endorsed ethic was one of asceticism and self-denial. St Paul was a Roman citizen and was educated in Greek philosophy. He made Christianity acceptable to the Romans by incorporating Greek philosophical ideas, especially the Platonic view of dualism. An outlook was presented based on a dualistic world-view: this world being one of necessary suffering, but preparation for a better world in the next life. Therefore, this world was inferior to the next world and the priests had turned Christianity into life denying, instead of Christ's life affirmation.

THE REVALUATION OF ALL VALUES

For Nietzsche, the declaration that 'God is dead' sets humans free to become their own person, to be the 'superman'. Their morality is a rejection of the herd morality. These are the elite; people who have mastered their own will to power and created life-affirming values to live by. The most crucial point for Nietzsche was that we should be life affirming. The superman, therefore, is one who realizes the potential of being a human being and is not consoled by a belief in the next life. The superman has mastered himself and creates his own values.

The practical implications of his philosophy are not something Nietzsche gave much consideration to. Nietzsche is not a democratic philosopher, for he is not a supporter of the values of the common herd. He believed in the great man, the hero, the superman who should be a law unto himself. However, it is difficult to see how a society that consisted of an elite that establishes their own values would function. They would look towards the masses with contempt and it is difficult to see how the supermen could either live amongst the masses or even amongst themselves. There would be inevitable conflict, although Nietzsche would have welcomed this provided it led to a revaluation of values.

Nietzsche's rejection of the Christian values, such as turning the other cheek, loving your neighbour and compassion for those that are suffering, might come across as somewhat callous. For one reason or another, many are unable to stand on their own two feet or face the realities of life and so there is a need for compassion. However, Nietzsche did not despise values such as compassion. It is the use of these values as a psychological prop, instead of looking towards one's own resources, that he disliked. Nietzsche's own almost crippling illness plagued him for most of his life, but the last thing he would have wanted was compassion or pity.

However, Nietzsche does seem too selective when talking about religion, asserting the negative while ignoring the variety of religious belief. Even if it were the case that Christianity is the cause of a slave morality, it has also been a vehicle of many revolutionary changes of which Nietzsche himself might approve. The same can be said of many other religions that Nietzsche would regard as 'life denying'.

Where does Nietzsche get *his* values? Nietzsche does not envision his superman as someone who is mean, vindictive or indiscriminately violent and cruel. Yet we must wonder *why not?* How can Nietzsche pick and choose the Superman's morality? Perhaps Nietzsche himself did not fully escape the values of his own religious upbringing.

* * *SUMMARY* * *

- Nietzsche's main concern was not whether beliefs are true or false, but why we believe what we do.

- He presents a genealogy of Christian morality, tracing it to the slaves of the Roman Empire.

- Christian morality is an expression of the will to power. Its values are based on the slaves' *ressentiment* towards their masters.

- The most important values for Nietzsche are those that affirm life. His criticism of Christian morality is that it rejects life and is based on hatred and fear.

9 Nietzsche's Legacy

Listen to me for I am thus and thus. Do not, above all, confound me with what I am not!

(Friedrich Nietzsche, *Ecce Homo*, Foreward)

1888

The year 1888 was the last year of Nietzsche's sane life and, ironically, the first of his fame. He spent the beginning of that fateful year in Nice and stayed in Turin from April till June, then he spent the summer in Sils-Maria, and then returned to Turin in September. It was, in this respect, a year of his usual wanderings. But, in other respects, it was very different. In his correspondence, Nietzsche reported that his health was improving and he felt a sense of joy and elation with life, not recognizing that these feelings of euphoria were symptomatic of forthcoming megalomania.

Added to this tragedy was the fact that Nietzsche was never to appreciate the success and influence his work was to have, for undoubtedly Nietzsche courted notoriety and wanted success. It was on the very first day of 1888 that the first ever review of Nietzsche's whole work appeared in a German newspaper. In April the internationally renowned Danish critic and biographer Georg Brandes (1842–1927) gave a series of successful lectures on Nietzsche at Copenhagen University. Nietzsche had finally arrived, yet his letters were becoming more and more bizarre and were evidence of the oncoming insanity.

In this final year, Nietzsche was as prolific a writer as ever. He wrote six short books: *The Wagner Case, The Twilight of the Idols, The Anti-Christ, Ecce Homo, Nietzsche contra Wagner*, and *Dithyrambs of Dionysus*. Are these works in any way a reflection of Nietzsche's imminent insanity? Nietzsche certainly does not introduce any new philosophy here and nor does he contradict what he has previously said. There is evident continuation from his previous work and the structure is generally tight and presented in a magnificent poetic style. These works deserve attention, therefore, and show no evidence of Nietzsche having lost his intellectual capacity. Quite the contrary, in fact. Here is a brief summary of the content of these works.

* *The Wagner Case* is essentially an attack on Wagner as a decadent and is actually quite a clever and amusing work.

* *Nietzsche contra Wagner* is another anti-Wagner pamphlet, although consisting mainly of sections from his earlier works that have been slightly modified. Nietzsche sees Wagner as the opposite of himself, but the kind of person Nietzsche would have become if he had not been stronger.

* *The Antichrist* is an attack on Christianity, the priests, and on St Paul especially; it states that only Jesus was the one true Christian.

* *Twilight of the Idols* is undoubtedly Nietzsche's finest book stylistically in this collection. Nietzsche writes glowingly of Goethe who he considers the prototype of the superman.

* Written only weeks before his collapse, *Ecce Homo* is another fierce attack upon Christianity. Nietzsche considers the Christian concept of God to be poisonous, and the teachings hostile to life. *Ecce Homo* is intelligent and witty, although Nietzsche's self-assessment, with chapter titles such as 'Why I Am So Clever' and 'Why I Write Such Excellent Books', could be an indication of megalomania or perhaps Nietzsche's clever use of irony!

* *Dithyrambs of Dionysus* consists of poems, some of which date back to *Zarathustra*.

1889

On the 3 January 1889, according to a well-known although possibly apocryphal account, Nietzsche walked out of his lodgings and saw a cabman beating his horse in the piazza. Nietzsche cried out, ran across the square and threw his arms around the neck of the horse. At that moment he lost consciousness. A crowd gathered and the landlord of Nietzsche's lodgings carried the still unconscious Nietzsche back to his room. When he finally came to he shouted, sang and punched away at the piano. When he calmed down he wrote a series of epistles to his friends and to the courts of Europe declaring that he, 'the Crucified', would be going to Rome in five days time and that all the princes of Europe and the Pope should assemble.

Nietzsche was now permanently insane. One of his few remaining friends, Overbeck, was disturbed by the letters and went to Turin. He persuaded Nietzsche to come to Basel. He was taken to a clinic in Jena, near the home of his mother. At the clinic, Nietzsche behaved like an imperious ruler, surveying the premises as if it was his palace. His conversation would switch from the rational to the nonsensical and violent at any given moment. When it was clear that no improvement was possible, Nietzsche was allowed to be housed with his mother at Naumburg. She looked after him devotedly until her death in 1897. For seven years she watched him night and day as he fell steadily into decline and apathy. It was unfortunate that, until his own death on 25 August 1900, the care of Nietzsche was to be in the hands of his sister Elizabeth.

ELIZABETH FÖRSTER-NIETZSCHE

Much of Nietzsche's legacy is closely related to his sister's less favourable legacy. Elizabeth Nietzsche, more than any other person, is responsible for the misunderstandings that have accompanied Nietzsche's philosophy to this day. When Nietzsche started writing poetry at the age of eight it was the six-year-old Elizabeth who collated the poems for him. At such an early age she already felt responsible for the work and life of the shy Friedrich.

Elizabeth loved the first Bayreuth Festival in 1876, the event that Nietzsche hated so much. She had already got to know Wagner through her brother and she was captivated by his anti-Semitic ideas. At the Festival she met and fell in love with Bernhard Förster, an anti-Semitic fanatic who was also addicted to Wagner's writings on Jews. Förster saw in Wagner a guide who would help him to become a professional anti-Semite, a member of the notorious 'German Seven' who called for the registration of Jews and the stop on Jewish immigration. Much to the disgust of Nietzsche, Förster married Elizabeth who, for her part, attempted unsuccessfully to recruit her brother into the anti-Semitic cause.

NEW GERMANY

Wagner once wrote of the possibility of establishing a pure German colony in South America where Jews would be banned. This idea, even though Wagner himself knew little about South America, was taken up by Bernhard Förster with great enthusiasm. He formed a group of somewhat disparate disciples and they, together with Elizabeth, sailed off to Paraguay where they established a colony called New Germany in 1887.

New Germany exists to this day, consisting of around 200 Germans (sharing 11 surnames). It continues to uphold the language, culture and practices of nineteenth-century German peasantry.

As for Bernhard Förster, he grew increasingly in debt and committed suicide the same year that Nietzsche went mad. Nietzsche's madness was the excuse Elizabeth needed to abandon New Germany to its fate and pursue her new full time mission of making her brother famous. For the next 40 years, Elizabeth manipulated his works and superimposed her own racist views upon them.

THE NIETZSCHE ARCHIVE

On returning to Germany, Elizabeth – who represented everything that Nietzsche hated about Germany and Germans – became his 'guardian' and owner of his copyrights. Immediately Elizabeth set about taking control of all of Nietzsche's writings. When Nietzsche collapsed he left behind mounds of unpublished material at his various lodgings. Elizabeth established an 'archive' in a house in Naumburg that would become a museum of Nietzsche works. Not only his works, however, but Nietzsche himself was lodged in a room as one of the exhibits. Incapable of coherent speech, he was exhibited to important visitors and dressed in a white robe like a Brahman priest. Elizabeth turned her brother into a prophet, surrounding him in mystique and turning his madness into something superhuman. Nietzsche had not gone mad at all, he had entered a higher plane!

In 1896 Elizabeth moved the growing archive to Weimar, which was considered the cultural centre of Germany. In fact, during World War II, Weimar was the centre for cultural propaganda. When the Russians occupied Weimar after the war, the archive was sealed off and remained so until the fall of the Berlin Wall in 1989.

The collected works of Nietzsche brought Elizabeth fame and fortune and she became the official mouthpiece for her brother. However, in collecting his works, she would ignore any of his philosophies that she disagreed with. She forged letters that she claimed Nietzsche had written to her that praised her, and wrote a popular biography of Nietzsche that was full of lies. The greatest sin of all was that she collected Nietzsche's unpublished notes into a book called the *Will to Power*. She claimed that this was Nietzsche's final testament, his true philosopyr. It is full of discarded thoughts and poorly written notes that Nietzsche had no intention of publishing. Although of historical interest, it is a shame that it is still quoted as an authority of Nietzsche's philosophy.

Nietzsche, at a time before his mental collapse and the fall out with his sister, had once written to Elizabeth requesting that, at his death – for he always believed he would die young – he should be given a pagan burial, with no priest at his grave. However, when he died on 25 August 1900, Elizabeth gave him a full Lutheran funeral and buried him in a coffin with a silver cross.

NIETZSCHE THE 'GERMAN NATIONALIST'

It has been said that Nietzsche was in no way a racist, except perhaps towards his own nation, the Germans. He hated what Germany had become; a nation of people who were nationalists, rather than 'good Europeans' and, worse, who were discriminatory towards others. It is a sad irony, therefore, that he was so praised by the German nationalists.

During World War I, Elizabeth Nietzsche proclaimed her brother as an imperialist and a warrior who would have been proud of the Germans' cause. She arranged for copies of *Thus Spoke Zarathustra* to be sent to the troops.

However, it was with the arrival of the dictators that she was really able to promote Nietzsche's philosophy. She heard that the Italian fascist dictator Mussolini had claimed that Nietzsche was a great influence on him, and so she made a point of establishing a regular correspondence with him. Mussolini took the notion of the superman to mean anyone who stands out from the crowd and controls his own destiny. In other words, he saw himself in this capacity. Elizabeth praised him as the new Caesar.

When Elizabeth chose to stage a play written by Mussolini at the archive, the Italian leader was unable to attend. However, the leader of the National Socialist Party, Adolph Hitler, did attend that night. This was her first introduction and she immediately fell under his spell. It was at the Bayreuth Festival on the 50th anniversary of Wagner's death that Elizabeth Nietzsche and Adolph Hitler discussed Nietzsche's philosophy. This resulted in Hitler giving his support to the archive. Although Nietzsche never became the official philosopher of Nazism, as this may have resulted in more people reading Nietzsche and realizing his true philosophy, many Nazi philosophers and academics liked to interpret Nietzsche as sympathetic towards the ideals of Nazism.

PHILOSOPHICAL INFLUENCE

Existentialism

Pick up virtually any introductory book on **existentialism** and it is likely that the first chapter will be on Friedrich Nietzsche. He is often regarded as the first existentialist and, when considering his philosophy, it is easy to see why he deserves this title. The philosophical movement of existentialism was popularized by

> **KEYWORD**
>
> Existentialism Philosophical movement that emphasizes human freedom.

the French philosopher Jean-Paul Sartre (1905–80). It is difficult to categorize existentialism because, by its very nature, it is against categorization. However, very generally, what all philosophers within this 'movement' share is an interest in human freedom, the belief that human beings have the innate capacity to choose freely their own courses of action and are not pre-destined in any way.

Much of Sartre's work echoes Nietzsche, agreeing with him that it is important to confront the fact that we now live in a godless world. Like Nietzsche, Sartre did not set out to prove that there was no God, but he was more concerned with considering the psychological, moral and political consequences of the acceptance of atheism. Although we have no fixed nature, the one thing we must all inevitably possess is freedom. Sartre stated that we are 'condemned to be free'. We have no choice but to be free, and to pretend otherwise is self-deception. Like Nietzsche, Sartre held that there is no 'objective' world, no hard facts, and no absolutes. The world as we understand it is one that we have imposed upon ourselves, not from outside of ourselves.

The analytic tradition

The **analytic** movement dominated philosophy in Britain and the United States for most of the second half of the twentieth century. Like existentialism, it is difficult to identify specific tenets of this movement, although most analytic philosophers argue that the primary aim of philosophy is, or should be, to look at how language is used. Language, it is argued, is the basis for all our knowledge and so when we use concepts the important thing is to consider how those concepts are used in the context of language.

KEYWORDS

Analytic The tradition in philosophy that emphasizes the importance of language in our understanding of the world.

Logical positivism An expression of the analytic tradition in philosophy. It argued that statements are meaningless if they cannot be verified.

One 'branch' of the analytic movement is called **logical positivism**. This adopted a criterion of meaning which stated that unless a statement can be verified by experience (for example, 'all bachelors are happy') or is true by definition (for example, 'a bachelor is an unmarried man') then it is *meaningless*. This inevitably results in metaphysical statements being discarded as irrelevant to philosophy because such statements as 'God is wise' cannot be proven by experience and nor is it by definition the case that 'God' and 'wisdom' are synonymous (although some have argued that in fact they *are* synonymous).

It is interesting that whereas existentialism tends to emphasize the irrational and emotional side, the analytic tradition is more rationalist and logical. Yet Nietzsche succeeds in straddling both traditions. Although it is difficult to say how much Nietzsche was a direct influence, much of his philosophy is within the positivist tradition, particularly his criticism of past philosophers for preoccupying themselves with metaphysical questions, and also his belief that it is not a matter of 'true' or 'false' but whether a claim makes sense that is important. Further, Nietzsche understood the importance of language in defining our world.

There have been many other philosophers and movements that can be traced back to Nietzsche, via the analytic tradition, continental philosophy and so on. More recently, the French philosopher Michel Foucault (1926–84) interpreted such things as punishment, sexuality, etc. as forms of the will to power. Even Nietzsche's writing style, originally condemned by scholars as lacking academic structure, has been imitated to an extent, most notably by Jacques Derrida (1930–), although the latter's style is more obscure.

OTHER INFLUENCES

The list, quite frankly, is virtually endless. In Russia, the symbolists who proclaimed art to be the new religion and the superman to be the artist adopted Nietzsche's philosophy. Nietzsche's future-orientated philosophy, of man as a 'bridge' to a higher man, influenced revolutionary thinkers such as Trotsky. In the literary world his influence on writers such as Thomas Mann, André Malraux, August Strindberg, George Bernard Shaw, R. M. Rilke, Joseph Conrad and Andre Gide has been pronounced. The theme of the anti-political individual who seeks perfection in isolation is particularly evident in the writings of Hermann Hesse. Sigmund Freud obviously had read Nietzsche, although he claimed not to be familiar with his works. The existentialist philosopher and novelist Albert Camus' last novel *The Fall* is an example of the will to power at work as the weak claim superiority by insisting that they are unworthy and guilt-ridden.

Nietzsche, no doubt, will continue to influence new generations on a variety of different levels. This could be due to his artistic style; the fact that a reader can pick on one profound sentence and write a novel around it. Or perhaps because his philosophy has outlived Nietzsche and his age, yet is just as applicable to today's society, if not more so.

✳ ✳ ✳ *SUMMARY* ✳ ✳ ✳

- 1888 was the last year of Nietzsche's sane life. It was a prolific period in terms of his writing.

- On 3 January 1889, Nietzsche broke down and remained insane for the rest of his life.

- Elizabeth Nietzsche returned to Germany and created an archive of Nietzsche's works. She did more than anyone else to ensure that Nietzsche became famous, however this was at the expense of a correct understanding of his philosophy.

- Nietzsche has been a great influence, not only in philosophy, but also in psychology and the arts.

- He died on 25 August 1900. Against Nietzsche's wishes, his sister gave him a full Christian burial.

GLOSSARY

amor fati meaning 'to love your fate'. A term Nietzsche used to express an affirmation of life.

analytic the tradition in philosophy that emphasizes the importance of language in our understanding of the world.

aphorism concise, pithy maxims varying in length from a single sentence to a short essay of several pages.

correspondence theory of truth the view that when we talk of things being 'true' then we are referring to things that actually exist in reality. When you point to an object and say 'it is there', then it *really is* there.

Darwinism a reference to the theories propounded by Charles Darwin (1809–82). Darwin is the founder of modern evolutionary theory.

dualism the philosophical position that there are two worlds: the physical and the non-physical

empiricism the philosophical position that we can acquire knowledge of the world through direct experience of the senses.

existentialism philosophical movement that emphasizes human freedom.

idealism stresses the importance of the mind in understanding what we can know about the world. At the most extreme, it argues that there is only the mind and no external world.

logical positivism an expression of the analytical tradition in philosophy. Argued that statements are meaningless if they cannot be verified.

metaphysics the speculation on what exists beyond the physical world, such as the existence of God, what is real, and so on.

monism the view that ultimately reality is composed of only one substance. It is, therefore opposed to dualism.

nihilism literally a 'belief in nothing', although there are varying levels of nihilism. At the less extreme it is a rejection of contemporary values and traditions, but does present the possibility of alternatives.

noumena metaphysical beliefs about the soul, the cosmos and God, that are matters of faith rather than of scientific knowledge.

pantheism the belief that there are not two worlds, but one and this is identified with God.

perspectivism the view that we perceive the world according to our perspective, although this may not be as the world actually is.

phenomena in Kantian terms, the world of everyday things that we can detect with our senses.

philology the study of langauge and literature.

pragmatic theory of truth the opposite of the correspondence theory of truth. Something is only 'true' to the extent that it is practical to believe in it.

rationalism the philosophical position that reason, the intellect, forms the basis for much of our knowledge.

relativism morals and beliefs are a product of a particular time and place and, therefore, there is no such thing as 'right' or 'wrong'.

ressentiment the French word for 'resentment'. Nietzsche uses it to explain his genealogy of morals. *Ressentiment* is the hostility that the slave feels towards the master.

FURTHER READING

Books written by Nietzsche

For dipping into, you might like to pick up a copy of *A Nietzsche Reader* (Penguin), edited and translated by R.J. Hollingdale, which divide Nietzsche's writings into themes. Another good read is *The Portable Nietzsche* (Viking Penguin), edited and translated by Walter Kaufmann This includes sections from Nietzsche's works, as well as his notes and letters.

Here is a selection of Nietzsche's works:

Faber, Marion (trans.) *Human, All Too Human*, Penguin (1994)

Hollingdale, R. J. (trans.) *Beyond Good and Evil*, Penguin (1990)
The translation by Marion Faber (Oxford Paperbacks, 1998) is also very good.

Hollingdale, R. J. (trans.) *Ecce Homo*, Penguin (1992)

Hollingdale, R. J. (trans.) *Thus Spoke Zarathustra*, Penguin (1969)

Hollingdale, R. J. (trans.) *Twilight of the Idols*, Penguin (1968)

Whiteside, Shaun (trans.) *The Birth of Tragedy*, Penguin (1993)

Books about Nietzsche and his work

The following are good general introductions to Nietzsche's life and work

Chamberlain, Lesley *Nietzsche in Turin*, Quartet Books (1997)
This presents a portrait of Nietzsche in the last year of his sane life.

Hollingdale, R. J. *Nietzsche*, Ark (2001)

Stern, J. P. *Nietzsche*, Fontana (1978)

Tanner, Michael *Nietzsche*, OUP (1994)

The following are more detailed commentaries on Nietzsche's work:

Danto, Arthur *Nietzsche as Philosopher*, Columbia University Press (1980) This examines Nietzsche's main themes.

Kaufmann, Walter *Nietzsche: Philosopher, Psychologist, Antichrist,* Princeton University Press (1974)
This is a detailed and ground-breaking examination of Nietzsche's philosophy.

Lampert, Laurence *Nietzsche's Task,* Yale University Press (2001)
This is a section-by-section commentary on *Beyond Good and Evil.*

Lampert, Laurence *Nietzsche's Teaching,* Yale University Press (1986)
This is an interpretation of *Thus Spoke Zarathustra.*

Myerson, George *Nietzsche's <u>Thus Spake Zarathustra</u> A Beginner's Guide,* Hodder & Stoughton (2001)
Offering a concise summary of the whole book with explanations of the most important themes.

CHRONOLOGY OF MAJOR WORKS

1871 *Birth of Tragedy*
1873 *Untimely Meditations I*
1874   *II, III*
1876   *IV*
1878 *Human, All Too Human*
1880 *The Wanderer and His Shadow*
1881 *Dawn*
1882 *The Gay Science*
1883 *Thus Spoke Zarathustra I, II*
1884   *III*
1885   *IV*
1886 *Beyond Good and Evil*
1887 *The Genealogy of Morals*
1889 *The Twilight of the Idols*
1889 *The Antichrist*
1889 *Ecce Homo*
1889 *Nietzsche contra Wagner*

INDEX

NIETZSCHE'S
THUS SPAKE ZARATHUSTRA
A BEGINNER'S GUIDE

George Myerson

With its many famous lines and statements – including the notorious news that 'God is dead!' – Nietzsche's *Thus Spake Zarathustra* has provoked and enthralled generations of readers. Literary masterpiece and angry polemic, manifesto and poem, personal confession and historic prophecy: what will you find in Nietzsche's visionary theory?

George Myerson's lively text:

- Investigates the background of *Thus Spake Zarathustra*

- Offers a clear and concise summary of the whole book

- Gives close-up explanations of the most important arguments

- Focuses on the central concepts for the reader such as the superman, redemption and eternal return.